"This book is a work of profound study of the Books of the Pentateuch (Genesis, Exodus, Leviticus, Numbers and Deuteronomy), and many other sources.

It is not only about music but also the work of a gifted and learned musician. Music has been a part of the human experience from the very beginning.

Music has to do with human emotions. It expresses joy and it expresses deep despair and everything in between.

At its summit, it is an expression of worship to the Almighty. At its lowest depth, it is to the glory of mankind or those who exalt themselves.

Let this be an offering to the glory of God Most High."

— **The Reverend David Heussler.**

WORSHIP IN THE BEAUTY OF HOLINESS

An Overview of The Pentateuch

LOIS SONSIE-BEEL

Published in Australia by Sid Harta Books & Print Pty Ltd,
ABN: 34632585293
23 Stirling Crescent, Glen Waverley, Victoria 3150 Australia
Telephone: +61 3 9560 9920, Facsimile: +61 3 9545 1742
E-mail: author@sidharta.com.au

First published in Australia 2023
This edition published 2024
Copyright © Lois Sonsie-Beel 2023
Cover design, typesetting: WorkingType (www.workingtype.com.au)

The right of Lois Sonsie-Beel to be identified as the
Author of the Work has been asserted in accordance with the
Copyright, Designs and Patents Act 1988.

All rights reserved. No part of this publication may be reproduced, stored in a retrieval system, or transmitted, in any form or by any means without the prior written permission of the publisher, nor be otherwise circulated in any form of binding or cover other than that in which it is published and without a similar condition being imposed on the subsequent purchaser.

ISBN: 978-1-922958-55-6 (paperback)
978-0-6486480-6-2 (ebook)

*I dedicate this book to Rosemary Cowtan
who has supported and encouraged me
throughout my musical career.*

Acknowledgements

At this point I would like to acknowledge the guidance and support I have received from Deanna Moodie, with whom I worked in close collaboration.

Deanna was able to assist me in three vital areas of my writing. Firstly, her personal faith in the God of creation, together with her deep understanding of the Bible as an accurate book of world history, and secondly, her musical studies which embrace piano, trombone, and a passion for praise and worship including hymns, have enabled her understanding of music throughout the ages. Lastly, Deanna's university studies have been pivotal in facilitating her in bringing together the many references required when writing a Biblical history book.

Although my training in both music and history have been extensive, Deanna has greatly enriched my knowledge as to how to present a book for publication.

Additionally, Neil Moodie (Deanna's husband) has been a support throughout the process, encouraging me with his technical support and his endless supply of humour.

My grateful thanks to both of you.

I also wish to thank the following people who contributed to the progress of this book: My late husband, Geoffrey, who bequeathed me a magnificent library, and my son, Dr Nathan Beel, who has always been on hand to question me if he felt my ideas and thoughts could be expressed more clearly.

Preface

An underlying motivation for my writing this book flows from a desire to understand God and His divine creation. We can only marvel that the genesis of God's work *In the beginning God created the heavens and the earth* (Genesis 1:1) has endured throughout the world today, even amid the evil and devastation around us.

I have sought to return to the 'beginning' to research the human journey in order to discover the many people who have worked to bring goodness, love, and advancement through their discoveries to countless lives throughout the ages.

Commencing at the beginning, I became aware that the Pentateuch revealed to me a relationship with the world as we know it today. These five books, Genesis, Exodus, Leviticus, Numbers, and Deuteronomy, together with other biblical references, completely cover the works of God and His creativity from prior to our existence to the present age.

One can be in awe at human endeavour and achievements from Creation to the present time! These questions could be asked: How could we mortals have created so many amazing edifices with such primitive tools? How could artists paint amazing pictures and mosaics throughout the centuries, with such a limited palette? How is it that the great works of literature and epic writings from prior to the invention of the printing press survived, not only during the period of Creation, and that much is still around for all to enjoy today?

I will seek to address these questions and many more as I explore the breathtaking musical achievements that have taken place throughout the ages.

Contents

1. The Heart of God	1
2. The Third Heaven	17
3. The Second Heaven	33
4. Archangels	51
5. Lucifer	69
6. Lucifer's Equipment	81
7. The Fall of Lucifer	97
8. The First Heaven	105
9. Creation of Humankind	117
10. The Creation	125
11. The Fall	143
12. Cain and Abel	151
13. Mesopotamia	165
14. The Call of Abraham	177
15. Building Bridges	191
16. Life in Egypt	211
17. Moses and the Exodus	221
18. Development of Behaviour and Worship	237
19. The Tabernacle	253
20. Israel's Religious Leaders	269
21. Ritual Patterns of Worship	293
22. Moses the Song Writer and Journalist-Historian	309
The Pentateuch	323
References	329

1. THE HEART OF GOD

His Love to All

> In the beginning God created
> the heavens and the earth.
> *(Genesis 1:1)*

When considering the commencement of a journey through history from a Christian point of view, the first step would be to seek to know and understand to a degree our Eternal God, from where all things in the heavens and on earth emanate. Often, people who believe in and pray to God have a limited idea of who He is, or how they can connect with Him through their faith and achieve seemingly impossible things. The Oxford University (2011) quotes: "God is a personal spiritual being beyond human understanding."

A leading truth is to recognise that God's presence and being is in control of all that He has created. The second wondrous truth is that men and women have been made in the image of God, thus reflecting His qualities as described in the Bible. As we consider these important truths, we can more fully understand and interpret ourselves as human beings and our place in the world.

Throughout the Bible, God has revealed Himself not only through creation, but also through His mighty deeds. One such mighty deed was the dividing of the Red Sea to allow the Israelites to pass to the other side in safety (Exodus 14:21). God has also gone by different names which reveal something about His character.

The great bard William Shakespeare wrote a soliloquy spoken by Juliet in the play *Romeo and Juliet* (act 2, scene 2), 'What is in a name? That which we call a rose by any other name would smell as sweet' (Shakespeare, 1595, as cited in Belsey, 2014). Although in this citation, a name may not have meant much to Juliet, the Bible shows repeatedly that a person's name often described something significant associated with the individual. A person's new name may describe their character, occupation, or a spiritual quality, which is supported by a Godly life.

As recorded in the Scriptures, a given name was changed when God ordained someone for a specific task. Often this was followed by an outpouring of the Holy Spirit.

Two instances of a God-given name change in the Old Testament are Abram and Jacob. Abram, meaning 'exulted father', was changed to Abraham, meaning 'father of many nations' (Genesis 17:3–5). This describes the outworking of a promise from God to Abraham and his descendants, expressed in the existence of the Jewish people. They have continued to survive through the centuries and in 1948 they became the nation of Israel. They are still in existence today.

The second instance occurred when Jacob wrestled with a man throughout the night, and refused to let go when morning came:

> So, Jacob was left alone, and a man wrestled with him
> till daybreak. When the man saw that he could not
> overpower him, he touched the socket of Jacob's hip so
> that his hip was wrenched as he wrestled with the man.
> Then the man said, "Let me go, for it is daybreak." But
> Jacob replied, "I will not let you go unless you bless me."
> *(Genesis 32:24–26)*

Prior to this encounter, Jacob had been considered an unlikely choice to be the embodiment of God's promises. After his wrestle with the mysterious stranger, his name changed from Jacob, figuratively meaning 'he grasps the heel', aptly describing his devious nature since supplanting his brother's inheritance. This changed man was determined to continue wrestling until he was blessed by the stranger, resulting in a new God-given name, Israel:

> The man asked him, "What is your name?" "Jacob",
> he answered. Then the man said, "Your name will no
> longer be Jacob, but Israel, because you have struggled
> with God and with humans and have overcome."
> *(Genesis 32:27–28)*

Further examples of name changes in the New Testament are Simon whom Christ named Peter, and Saul whose name was changed to Paul. Throughout the Scriptures God has revealed his names to his chosen ones, names which have expressed the Lord's purpose as to the particular task he had in mind for them.

The first recorded name of God in the Hebrew and Christian Scriptures in Genesis 1:1 (Amplified Bible) is *Elohim*:

> In the beginning God (Elohim) created [by forming from nothing] the heavens and the earth.

Elohim means God, which indicates His might. The two words in this phrase are 'El', referring to the character of God, and 'Olam', signifying forever, continuous, and everlasting, which together affirm God's existence from eternity to eternity.

The second name of God recorded is *Eternal God*, which appears in Genesis 21:33 when Abraham was in Beersheba:

> Abraham planted a tamarisk tree in Beersheba, and there he called on the name of the Lord, the Eternal God.

The third name relevant here is *Yahweh*, a personal name for God meaning *Jehovah*. Yahweh indicates the only true Lord God, master, and creator of all things, who is holy and ever-present. The Lord revealed this name to the Israelites through Moses in Exodus 3:13–15:

> Moses said to God, "Suppose I go to the Israelites and say to them, 'The God of your fathers has sent me to you,' and they ask me, 'What is his name?' Then what shall I tell them?" God said to Moses, "I AM WHO I AM. That is what you will say to

them, I AM has sent me to you ... This is my name forever, the name you will call me from generation to generation."

A first-century Romano-Jewish historian and military leader, Flavius Josephus (1989) observed:

> Now Moses, since he had heard and seen Him, requested that He would also tell him His name, whereupon God declared to him His holy name, which had never been discovered to men before. Concerning which it is not lawful for me to say any more.

The name *Yahweh* was strongly associated with the third commandment whereby God emphasised His holiness and the respect due to Him and His name:

> You shall not misuse the name of the Lord your God [Yahweh], for the Lord will not hold anyone guiltless who misuses his name.
> *(Exodus 20:7)*

Around one thousand years later, during the Hellenistic period, Jews refrained from pronouncing or writing the name *Yahweh* in fear of accidently blaspheming. While the Jews of this time may have been overly cautious, they showed reverence for the holiness of God's proper name. The essence and the intention of the third commandment is still applicable to every person today, requiring each to show due respect to the Eternal Creator.

So far, the focus has been on understanding God and His attributes; however, many Bible passages describe Him not only as Eternal Spirit, but also the one who continues to guide the lives of all His creatures.

When Abraham was tested to the extreme by the request of God that he be willing to sacrifice his beloved son Isaac, who asked of him, *"Where is the Lamb?"*, Abraham replied to Isaac, saying, *"God himself will provide a lamb for the burnt offering, my son."* After sacrificing a lamb, Abraham called the place *Jehovah Jireh*, meaning *The Lord Will Provide* (Genesis 22:7–8, 14).

In a later incident, after supplying water for the Israelites at the commencement of the wilderness journeys, God gave this promise:

> If you listen carefully to the Lord your God and do what is right in His eyes, I will not bring on you any of the diseases I brought on the Egyptians, for I am the Lord who heals you [Jehovah Rapha].
> *(Exodus 15:26)*

The words *Jehovah Rapha* are used some sixty times in the Old Testament, and mean 'to restore/repair, heal, and cure physically, emotionally and spiritually' (Compelling Truth, 2021; MVM, 2014).

When King Hezekiah became ill to the point of death, he prayed for healing and God answered him:

> The Lord says, "I have heard your prayer and have seen your tears; I will heal you ... I will add fifteen years to your life ..." and he [Hezekiah] recovered.
> *(2 Kings 20:5–7)*

In Matthew 8:3 the New Testament records John's vision of a man with leprosy:

> Jesus reached out his hand and touched the man. "I am willing," he said. "Be clean!" Immediately he was cleansed of his leprosy.

Revelation 21:4 then extends Christ as the healer – *Jehovah Rapha* – into our heavenly existence:

> He will wipe every tear from their eyes, there will be no more death or mourning or crying or pain.
> *(Revelation 21:4)*

C. Michael Hawn (as cited in Discipleship Ministries, 1867/2013) proposed these questions:
- How do you express the inexpressible mystery of the Creator whose name was unutterable in the Hebrew Scripture save the self-described I AM?
- How do you put into words what cannot be known?
- How do you sing about the One who is ineffable – beyond all words?

Theologians throughout the centuries have attempted to answer these questions by referring to three key names as descriptors based on the Biblical principles of God's qualities. The first being omnipotent, as used in Revelation, with the second and third descriptors being omniscient and omnipresent, terms which help us understand the essence of God more fully.

Omnipotent – almighty

The Greek word translated as omnipotent here, is 'pantocrator', meaning 'all ruling' and 'almighty', which affirms God's authority and rulership over all creation, together with His legitimate authority originating from Him.

King David exults God's omnipotence in Psalm 135:5-7:

> I know that the Lord is great, that our Lord is greater than all gods. The Lord does whatever pleases him, in the heavens and on the earth, in the seas and all their depths. He makes clouds rise from the ends of the earth; he sends lightning with the rain and brings out the wind from his storehouses.

The word omnipotent is included in Revelation 19:6 in the New King James Version (NKJV):

> Alleluia! For the Lord God Omnipotent reigns!

When George Frideric Handel (1685-1759) wrote 'Messiah', he included the 'The Hallelujah Chorus'. Based on the above verse, and other verses from Revelation, this chorus announces the might and power of God and His Christ. The Hallelujah

1. The Heart of God

Chorus has become a favourite anthem. During Christmas particularly, the Hallelujah Chorus celebrations throughout the world ring with praise and adulation to God:

> Hallelujah! For the Lord God omnipotent reigneth
> Hallelujah! The kingdom of this world
> Is become the kingdom of our Lord and of His Christ
> And He shall reign for ever and ever
> King of kings and Lord of lords
> And He shall reign for ever and ever.
> Hallelujah!
> *(Revelation 19:6; 11:15; 19:16)*

A short excerpt from the book entitled *The Great Composers* (MC, 1983) claims:

> This has been described as the most famous chorus in all classical music, wonderful in its simplicity and boldness of effect. Although unnecessary, a tradition which is often continued today, stems from a performance at which George II rose to his feet in an acknowledgement that God and his Christ are Lord of all. The audience followed the king and rose to their feet, and they all remained standing until the chorus ended.

Omniscient – all-knowing

The Lord is omniscient, all-knowing from eternity to eternity, yet as mortals we are locked in a timespan, making it almost impossible to foretell or forthtell to any significant degree.

As qualities of the eternal God, omniscience together with omnipotence were inseparable in creation. In concert with his power and might, God's control of all things presupposes knowledge of all things relating to the works of creativity:

> Known unto God are all His works
> from the beginning of the world.
> *(Acts 15:18 KJV)*

This knowledge includes even the minutest details:

> Indeed, the very hairs of your head are all numbered.
> *(Matthew 10:30)*

The Collins English Dictionary (2021) also offers this definition of the term omniscient: "Having complete or unlimited knowledge, awareness, or understanding, perceiving all things." Furthermore, Isaiah spoke of God as declaring the end from the beginning:

> I make known the end from the beginning, from ancient times, what is still to come; My purpose will stand, and I will do all that I please.
> *(Isaiah 46:10)*

Human beings are capable of perceiving much of their surroundings through their senses; however, there are limits to what their senses can comprehend. Throughout the Psalms, David continually wrote of God's eternal power and knowledge of his own existence. Psalm 139 develops this theme:

> You have searched me, Lord, and you know me.
> You know when I sit and when I rise;
> you perceive my thoughts from afar.
> You discern my going out and my lying down;
> you are familiar with all my ways.
> Before a word is on my tongue,
> you, Lord, know it completely.
> You hem me in behind and before,
> and you lay your hand upon me.
> Such knowledge is too wonderful for me,
> too lofty for me to attain.
> *(Psalm 139:1–6)*

Omnipresent – ever-present

God is omnipresent because he is present all the time and simultaneously throughout the whole of creation. He is everywhere! This is reflected in the Biblical teaching that there is no physical location in the universe that is not under God's authority; therefore, it is futile for anyone to hide from God. The earliest example of this is found in Genesis 3:8 where, after eating the forbidden fruit, Adam and Eve tried in vain to hide from God.

Following David's recognition of God's omniscience and in his quest to know the Lord at a deeper level, he moved effortlessly into God's omnipresence by posing a question-and-answer dialogue with the Almighty, reaffirming his belief that God is everywhere, in the known and unknown universe:

> Where can I go from your Spirit? Where can I flee from your presence? If I go up to the heavens, you are there; if I make my bed in the depths, you are there. If I rise on the wings of the dawn, if I settle on the far side of the sea, even there your hand will guide me, your right hand will hold me fast.
> *(Psalm 139:7–10)*

Indeed, the Spirit of God is infinite!

These attributes of God have inspired the saints of God throughout the ages. Theophilus of Antioch (170 AD, as cited in Kirby, 2022) supplied an expanded description of God's omnipresence:

> But this is the attribute of God, the Highest and Almighty, and the living God, not only to be everywhere present, but also, to see all things and to hear all, and by no means to be confined in a place; for if He were, then the place containing Him would be greater than He, for that which contains is greater than that which is contained. For God is not contained but is Himself the place of all.

Hymn Writers

Hymn writers and poets have continued to give comfort and inspiration to many people as they have portrayed through their prose, verse, and music, glimpses of the Eternal God and His creative powers. Like the psalmists of old, hymn writers hail from all walks of life throughout the world, and are united in their adoration of Creator God and His Son.

The hymn 'Immortal, Invisible, God Only Wise' (Smith, 1867/2012) encapsulates much of God's divine characteristics. Based on verse 17 in 1 Timothy 1, Walter Chalmers Smith (1824 –1908) successfully provided a deeper insight into this amazing phenomenon.

Smith, a Scottish Free Church minister was educated at the Universities of Aberdeen and Edinburgh, served in London and Edinburgh, and was elected moderator of the General Assembly in 1893. He wrote many hymns, with 'Immortal, Invisible, God Only Wise' remaining popular today. It is usually sung to the tune 'St Denio', originally a Welsh ballad, and became a hymn under the name Palestrina.

The central theme of light showing the transcendence of the one known as 'I AM' is constantly referenced throughout the hymn. Stanza one refers to the eternal one as 'light inaccessible hid from our eyes.'

In stanza two the holy one is described as 'silent as light', and it reveals that this holy one rules in might. His justice can also be compared to the mountains which soar above, and goodness and love are reflected in the clouds that sustain life on earth.

Stanza three continues to expand more of His holy nature,

the source of all life to both great and small. The Lord is unchangeable, which is the antithesis of created creatures who blossom and flourish, then wither and perish.

Stanza four invites us all to continue the theme of light by joining in worship and praise to our great and mighty God, 'All praise we would render; Oh, help us to see, 'Tis only the splendour of light hideth Thee!'

Considering the holiness, love, and life, together with all the other attributes of the Lord of creation, is awesome yet humbling. Conversely, God, knowing the past, present, and future, encourages us to rely on Him who knows every detail of everything, trusting Him to influence events outside of our control. It can also help us be aware of our accountability to Him, as nothing we do is secret from Him.

1. The Heart of God

IMMORTAL, INVISIBLE, GOD ONLY WISE

Immortal, Invisible, God only wise,
In light inaccessible hid from our eyes,
Most blessed, most glorious, the Ancient of Days,
Almighty, victorious, thy great name we praise.

Unresting, unhasting, and silent as light,
Nor wanting, nor wasting, thou rulest in might;
Thy justice like mountains high soaring above
Thy clouds, which are fountains of goodness and love.

To all life thou givest, to both great and small;
In all life thou livest, the true life of all;
We blossom and flourish as leaves on the tree,
And whither and perish, but nought changeth thee.

Great Father of glory, pure Father of light,
Thine angels adore Thee, all veiling their sight;
All praise we would render; Oh, help us to see
'Tis only the splendour of light hideth Thee.

Conclusion

Having sought to provide an understanding of this eternal, invincible God, we will now move on to consider where God lives. Many believers and unbelievers alike think God dwells in heaven. As the word heavens is plural in the Bible, the idea of many heavens has been considered throughout the world from time immemorial.

> Now unto the King eternal, immortal, invisible, the only wise God, be honour and glory forever and ever.

2. THE THIRD HEAVEN

As one studies and reads of the amazing human achievements accomplished throughout history, the thought may be developed into these questions: Where did these ideas originate? Were they purely the result of the human creativity and endeavours, or were they in existence from eternity to eternity?

These questions, with many more, can be answered in the affirmative. All love, goodness, expertise, all giftedness, came into being from our God prior to our existence. He continues to demonstrate His power and creativity through His glorious kingdom, also known as heaven.

The Bible gives various references to heavenly places without supplying exhaustive descriptions. The first reference is found in Deuteronomy where we read:

> To the Lord your God belong the heavens,
> even the highest heavens, the earth and everything in it.
> *(Deuteronomy 10:14)*

The Rabbinic literature of Palestine in the early centuries of the first millenium AD , tried to define a more thorough explanation of the heavenly bodies, being influenced by the Ancient Greeks who believed in seven heavens. The Jews discussed this concept in the *Tractate Chagigah*, which made up the six orders of the Mishnah, a collection of Jewish oral traditions which is included in the *Talmud*.

All seven heavens are named as being terms or part-terms for God's dwelling place, and we find the seven heavens in the second of the six orders of the Moed (Festivals). More recently, most Christians agree that these are meaningful synonyms to explain an idea or situation, as only one appears to refer to a specific heaven. The following are the names of these seven heavens, which the *Talmud* (2022) considers make up the universe:

- Velum – the curtain of day and night (Isaiah 40:22)
- Expanse – the firmament (Genesis 1:17)
- Aether – where the Manna is made (Psalm 78:24–25)
- Habitation – where Michael stands at the altar (1 Kings 8:3)
- Dwelling Place – where the angels sing (Psalm 42:8)
- Fixed Residence – the dwelling place (1 Kings 8:39)
- Araboth – these are the souls of the righteous (Psalm 49:15).

Heaven's Location and Form

Another question may be posed: Where are these heavenly places?

The Bible indicates that the heavens are real places, and that they are above, that is, around the whole of the earth: *For as high as the heavens are above the earth, so great is His love for those who fear Him* (Psalm 103:11). Also, from which God comes down to earth: *No one has ever gone into heaven except one who came from heaven* (John 3:13).

There are forty-five verses in the Bible which describe resurrections; the following are three explicit examples:

> Jesus said to her, "I am the resurrection and the life. The one who believes in me will live, even though they die, and whoever lives by believing in me will never die."
> *(John 11:25)*

Although the Bible does not specify the exact location, and neither does it specify the form of the resurrection, whether physical, spiritual, or a combination of both, it could be argued that it is a spiritual dimension in which God is Spirit. Yet, on the other hand, the resurrection is always spoken of as a physical location, given that Christ's resurrection was physical.

> Now Mary stood outside the tomb crying. As she wept, she bent over to look into the tomb and saw two angels in white, seated where Jesus' body had been, one at the head and one at the foot. At this she turned around and saw Jesus standing there, but she did not realise that it was Jesus. Jesus said to her, "Mary! Go instead to my brothers and tell them I am ascending to my Father and your Father, to my God and your God."
> *(John 20:11–12, 14, 16–17)*

When Christ comes again, there will be a resurrection of all believers. Irrespective of its precise form, the emphasis of the Bible is that the heavens exist and are real.

The Three Heavens

Lockyer (1995) considers, along with others, that references in the Bible suggest that for our understanding, the heavens can be divided into three places, each a specific place for a specific activity. Dr Arno C. Gaebelein (1997) in his book *What the Bible Says About Angels*, proposed:

> In the Hebrew, heaven is plural, heavens. The Bible speaks of three heavens; the third heaven is of heavens, the dwelling place of God, where his throne has always been, the first heaven is considered by many as a place beyond the immediate heaven of the earth's atmosphere, in between these places is the second heaven where the stars and planets are situated and leads into the presence of God (p. 21).

In keeping with Gaebelein's idea, we will accept the idea that these three heavens do exist. Rather than commencing with the first heaven, which is the earth and its environs, we will begin with the third heaven. This is the central abode of God, where his most intimate creativity is displayed, and from where it flows to the second and first heavens.

The Bible has several verses referring to the third heaven. In the New Testament, Paul appears to describe a personal experience in his letter to the Corinthians: *I know a man in Christ who was caught up to the third heaven* (2 Corinthians 12:2). In his letter to the Ephesians, he describes Christ's ascension to heaven saying: *He who descended is the very one who ascended higher than all heavens, in order to fulfil the whole universe* (Ephesians 4:1).

God's Dwelling Place

Many men of God were privileged to enter the Holy Place, among whom were Moses, Ezekiel, Isaiah, John, and Satan. Apart from Satan, these men wrote vivid descriptions of what they saw including dwellings, activities, worship, and music. They also described the Holy Place as a place of divine glory, the place where the angels gathered, the place of the blessed dead. One day the angels came to present themselves before the Lord, and Satan also came with them (Job 1:6).

The first description of God in His abode was recorded in Exodus, when Moses, Aaron, Nadab, Abihu, and the seventy elders of Israel went up onto the mountain.

> They saw the God of Israel. Under his feet was
> something like a pavement made of lapis lazuli
> [sapphire], as bright blue as the sky.
> *(Exodus 24:10)*

The verse describes a vision experienced by multiple people simultaneously. It positions God in His abode and brings focus to both the substance of the pavement and the colour. This is quite a contrast to the Israelites' experience of ochre-coloured pavements made from straw and mud under oppressive conditions, and may reveal God's preference for fine quality materials, bright lively colour, and light. In ancient times, blue was a colour denoting wealth and power, and was also used in the tabernacle (Exodus 28:18).

God's Dwelling Place

In Revelation 21, John gives us the most vivid and graphic description of a city, portraying it as made of gold. Surrounding this was a high wall made of clear jasper, with twelve gates each made of a single pearl. These gates were placed on each side of the wall, upon which were written the twelve tribes of Israel. There were also twelve angels; three of these were located at each gate.

It is interesting to note that Ezekiel, hundreds of years earlier, described the twelve tribes of Israel from his vision of the future city of God, written on the gates of this city. He noted that there are three gates on each side, upon which are named the tribes of Israel (Ezek. 48:30–34).

- North side – gates of Reuben, Judah, and Levi
- East side – gates of Joseph, Benjamin, and Dan
- South side – gates Simeon, Issachar, and Zebulun
- West side – gates of Gad, Asher, and Naphtali.

> The name of the city from that time on
> will be the Lord is there.
> *(Ezekiel 48:35)*

The wall had twelve foundations each decorated with a precious stone: jasper, sapphire, agate, emerald, onyx, ruby, chrysolite, beryl, topaz, turquoise, jacinth, and amethyst, upon which were recorded the names of the twelve apostles of the Lamb . Here we see Israel with the Apostles, who were chosen to carry God's name to the world (Revelation 21:14).

Passing through the gates, John witnessed that *the streets of gold were like transparent glass* (Revelation 21:21). Moving on, the beauty of the light of God is further reflected and refracted from the facets of all the jewels that adorned the city. What a glorious place, where light flooded everywhere! It displays how much our Lord loves beauty and colour, which He has passed on to His children.

Mansions

The Lord Jesus added another element to the city of God, which is relevant to each believer today, as it was when He spoke these words of comfort to His disciples during His incarnation. He said:

> Let not your hearts be troubled, in my father's house are many mansions (dwelling places), if it were not so, I would have told you. I go to prepare a place for you.
> *(John 14:1–2 KJV)*

Here Jesus introduces us to a particularly important element in the city of our God. This is a promise as well as a personal avowal which relates to every person on earth no matter where they live. Our homes, whether large or small, are part of our habitation on earth which we understand. They are our protection where we can feel safe and secure, away from all that is happening outside. A place we can gather with our friends and family and be ourselves. Here Jesus assures us that in heaven a dwelling is even now waiting for our entry.

The Throne Room of God

The central point of the third heaven, or inner court, is the Royal Throne Room. This is where the Lord shines in his glory and surrounding him are twenty-four elders and angels (Revelation 4).

From the commencement of the Old Testament right to the visions at the end of the New Testament, godly men were given the privilege of peering into this inner court of heaven. These men, Isaiah, Ezekiel, Micaiah, and John, all described God sitting upon His glorious throne.

Micaiah

> I saw the LORD sitting on his throne with all the multitudes of heaven standing around him on his right and on his left.
> *(1 Kings 22:19; 2 Chronicles 18:18)*

Daniel

Daniel suffered much in his time in Babylon, being used by the Lord to carry his messages both present and future. During one of his visions, the Lord revealed himself to Daniel on a throne in heaven:

> As I looked, thrones were set in place, and the Ancient of Days took his seat. His clothing was as white as snow; the hair of His head was white like wool. His throne was flaming with fire, and its wheels were all ablaze. A river of fire was flowing, coming out from before Him. Thousands upon thousands attended Him; ten thousand times ten thousand stood before Him.
> *(Daniel 7:9–10)*

The Orthodox Christian hymns and symbols, as well as the western church, recognise the term 'Ancient of Days' as God the Father.

Isaiah

One of the most evocative verses in the Old Testament is recorded by Isaiah when he describes his vision of God in the heavens:

> In the year that King Uzziah died, I saw the Lord, high and exalted, seated on a throne; and the train of his robe, filled His temple. Above him were seraphim, each with six wings.
> *(Isaiah 6:1–2)*

Ezekiel

Writing during the time of Isaiah again places the focus on the throne itself, describing it as being made of blue sapphire. Ezekiel saw:

Above the vault over their heads was what looked like a throne of lapis lazuli [sapphire], and high above on the throne was a figure like that of a man... as if full of fire; and brilliant light surrounded him. Like the appearance of a rainbow in the clouds on a rainy day, so was the radiance around him. This was the appearance of the likeness of the glory of the Lord.
(Ezekiel 1:26–28)

John

As John was praying in his cave on the Isle of Patmos, he exclaimed:

At once I was in the Spirit, and there before me was a throne in heaven with someone sitting on it, and the one who sat there had the appearance of jasper and ruby. A rainbow that shone like an emerald encircled round the throne. Surrounding the throne were twenty-four other thrones and seated on them were twenty-four elders. They were dressed in white and had crowns of gold on their heads.
(Revelation 4:2–4)

As with other visions, each emphasised different elements as to what they saw. This is not unusual, as the people tended to interpret what they saw in different ways, although there are many similarities. Isaiah saw the Lord high and lifted up; Ezekiel described a throne of sapphire; Micaiah glimpsed the host of heaven by his side; and John saw a great white throne. Each person experienced the glory and majesty of God.

Heavenly Activities

The Scriptures also hold references to created beings who inhabit this place. These beings are called angels. Heaven is not only a place filled with God's glory, but also a busy place where angels are able to enter and leave at will attending to their countless activities. These activities are primarily expressed in praising and extolling God.

Heaven is also filled with musicians of the highest degree, expertly created by the eternal God himself. Every musician continuously performs the heavenly songs day and night:

> They sang the song of Moses... and the song of the Lamb:
> "Great and marvellous are your deeds,
>
> Lord God Almighty. Just and true are your ways,
>
> King of the nations. Who will not fear you, Lord, and bring glory to your name? For you alone are holy. All nations will come and worship before you, for your righteous acts have been revealed."
> *(Revelation 15:3-4)*

The singers around the throne of God were accompanied by musical instruments, appearing to negate the thought that the instruments were the result of human endeavour. *The sound*

I heard was like that of harpists playing their harps (Revelation 14:2). Other instruments recorded here are the trumpets. *And I saw the seven angels who stand before God, and seven trumpets were given to them* (Revelation 8:1–2). *And they sang a new song before the throne* (Revelation 14:3). Throughout the book of Revelation there appear numerous beautiful new songs, many which have been reproduced throughout history and are still sung today.

The River of Life

Flowing down the middle of this city was the river of life which had trees laden with much fruit and leaves on either side for the healing of the nations. Rivers and streams have appealed to the human heart and imagination from time immemorial.

> Then the Angel showed me the river of life, as crystal,
> flowing from the throne of God and of the lamb.
> *(Revelation 22:1)*

Thousands of years prior to John's vision, a music director began Psalm 46 with an affirmation that God is our refuge and strength. He continued by placing before us a vivid scene of upheaval in the natural world, with mountains quaking and falling, together with waters raging. He then experienced a similar vision to the one that John saw in the heavens, portraying not chaos but peace and beauty.

2. The Third Heaven

> There is a river whose streams make glad the city of God,
> the Holy Place where the Most High dwells.
> *(Psalm 46:4)*

Christians throughout the ages have been enriched by these thoughts. Many poets have united with the psalmists by continuing this theme describing God's people gathering at the river, where they experienced God's blessing on their lives in times of darkness.

One such poet, in a desperate time in his life, raised his eyes to the heavens and was not only given the courage to continue but also was inspired to write a hymn for the occasion. Robert Lowry (1826–1899) was the writer and composer of the hymn , 'Shall we gather at the river?', which is still a favourite today.

Lowry was also a minister of the Baptist church, and he later joined the staff of Bucknell University, Lewisburg, Pennsylvania as a lecturer of literature. In 1864, during his tenure as minister of Hanson Place Baptist Church, Brooklyn, New York, two cataclysmic events were taking place. The American civil war and an epidemic that was raging throughout the city bringing death to people everywhere.

During this time, he was either visiting members of his congregation or providing them with the essentials to survive. While in his exhausted state, he experienced a vision of the future as it passed before him, in which he forecast the apocalypse based on John's vision . It was in the form of a montage in three parts: God's throne at its brightest, the heavenly river of life, and the gathering of the saints.

In his heart, Lowry questioned the hymn-writers whose focus was often based on the river of death, saying little about the river of life that flowed out of the throne of God and of the Lamb. As he considered this, the words came as a question, 'Shall we gather at the river?' The answer was 'Yes'.

SHALL WE GATHER AT THE RIVER?

Shall we gather at the river?
Where bright angels' feet have trod.
With its crystal tide forever
Flowing from the throne of God.

Yes, we'll gather at the river,
The beautiful, the beautiful river.
Gather with the saints at the river
That flows from the throne of God.

Soon we'll reach the shining the river,
Soon our pilgrimage will cease.
Soon our happy hearts will quiver
With a melody of peace.

Yes, we'll gather at the river,
The beautiful, the beautiful river.
Gather with the saints at the river
That flows from the throne of God.

Conclusion

It is amazing that believers throughout the ages have had a sense of being part of a triune existence – the past, the present, and the future. We are very aware of the past, because all things that were in the heavenly places have been, and are still being, replicated in the post-creation of humankind.

We also live in the hope of our future, when so much of what we read in the Bible will become a reality.

We will now explore more fully those beings who are with the Lord from eternity to eternity. The angels are part of our existence and support upon earth.

The following is a suitable verse to take with us as we move on to the next chapter:

> The city does not need the sun
> or the moon to shine on it,
> for the glory of God gives it light
> and the lamb is its lamp.

3. THE SECOND HEAVEN
Stars and Angels

Many Christians believe that the Bible is difficult and arduous to read throughout, so they concentrate on portions with which they are familiar. However, this practice of Bible study denies the opportunity to grasp many aspects of the eternal God and His heavenly places.

Created Beings

There are 273 references to angels in the Scriptures: 108 in the Old Testament, and 165 in the New Testament, of which 57 are in the book of Revelation.

The Bible reveals that together with our place on earth, it is possible that the angels may have their abode among the stars, the second heaven – the stellar heaven, home of the angels. Isaiah 14:13 appears to confirm an intermediary place between the first heaven and a third heaven, where Satan is described as saying in his heart: I will ascend to the heavens; I will raise my throne above the stars of God.

In the New Testament, Paul refers to other beings apart from humans, who also reside in the heavens:

> All flesh is not the same, there are heavenly bodies and there are earthly bodies, a natural body, and a spiritual body.
> *(2 Corinthians 15:39)*

The differences are a reality – the angels are spiritual and heavenly beings, while we humans are mortal and earthly. They are identified as angels, which is an official title, *nomen officii*, describing the essence of the angels. Throughout the Bible, the angels are identified by their service to God and humankind.

In addition, stars have been used as a poetic way of speaking of angels. This is evident when God spoke to Job in Job 38:4,6–7, reminding him who created the earth: *Where were you when I laid the earth's foundation, or who laid the cornerstone, while the morning stars sang together, and all the angels shouted for joy.* This symbolic belief is continued in Revelation when *the stars were there with the seven angels of destruction* (Revelation 1–3).

The *New Illustrated Bible Dictionary* (Thomas Nelson, 1995) explains:

> Stars are a generic term for any heavenly bodies visible in the night sky. This includes stars, planets, comets and meteors, but excludes the sun and the moon. The host of heaven sometimes refers to all the astronomical phenomena visible in the night skies.

Angels are also described as lesser deities in all heathen mythologies, which also presume the existence of a higher order of beings between God and humankind, superior to humans and inferior to God. These mythologies presuppose that together with such beings, there are also supernatural places described throughout that are real.

Many believers through the ages have confidently believed that angels not only serve God in His heavenly abode, but also act as messengers who intervene in the affairs of men. Although these beings are 'genderless', angels often appeared to project themselves to humans who experienced a vision, in a manner that they could understand.

These appearances took on a human form and are called 'Anglophones'. When these epiphanies were recorded in the Scriptures, they were often mistaken as men because of their man-like appearance.

Abraham made this error when he looked up and saw three men standing nearby near the tree of Mamre (Genesis 18:1). On another occasion the Lord sent an angel to Hagar. God heard Ishmail, son of Hagar, crying and the Angel of God called to Hagar from heaven and said to her: *What is the matter, Hagar? Do not be afraid: God has heard the boy crying as he lies there* (Genesis 21:17).

A further appearance occurred when an angel manifested himself in human form to Balaam, on his way to meet the Moabite officials (Numbers 22:24).

Together, with references in the Bible regarding angels, many of our great church leaders over the centuries have also recorded their thoughts and faith regarding angels. Three are listed below together with their quotes.

St Augustine of Hippo (354–430 AD) , a theologian, philosopher, and bishop, described the spiritual difference of angels when he wrote:

> The angels are spirits, but it is not because they are spirits that they are angels. They become angels when they are sent.

For the name angels refers to their office, not their nature. You ask the name of this nature, it is spirit; you ask its office, it is that of an angel 'messenger'. In as far as he exists, as angels, he is a spirit, in as far as he acts, he is an angel.

We move through the centuries to learn what Martin Luther (1483–1546) said about the angels. He saw them in particular for our benefit, upon earth. He writes (cited in Luther's AZ Quotes 2022):

Angels are our true and trusty servants, performing offices and works that one poor miserable mendicant would be ashamed to do for another. Angels are spiritual creatures, created by God, without any body for the service of Christendom, and the Church.

From Lockyer (1995), we learn that although there is no specific doctrine of angels found in the Bible, as there is for God, Jesus Christ, the Holy Spirit, and human beings, angels appear everywhere from Genesis to Revelation. In both the Old and New testaments, the root word for angel means 'messenger'.

In the Old Testament, the Hebrew word is *mal'akh*, and in the New Testament the Greek word is *angelos*. Both definitions, in each language, denote 'messenger', whether human or divine.

Time of Creation

Angels did not always exist. God, the Creator, created them just as he created humans and all else on earth. But a question may be asked, 'When and where did angels come from?' The Bible does not give us a direct answer, although we know they were present when God created the earth, as we see in Job 38:7: *While the morning stars sang together, and all the angels shouted for joy?* This appears to indicate that before the creation of the heavens and earth as we know it, angels were inhabiting the great expanse of the heavens.

Similarities Between Angels and Humans

Lightner (1998) points out that angels and humans have many similarities. He says:

- angels and humans were created in a state of perfection, as all that God made, God had pronounced 'good'
- angels and humans have been given personalities
- angels and humans sinned against God
- angels and humans followed the example of Satan in his great sin of pride and rebellion against God (Isaiah 14:13–14)
- humankind sinned through Adam (Genesis 3; Romans 5:15)
- neither angels nor humans are to be worshipped
- angels and humans are to serve humankind and be servants of the Most High God.

Naming the Angels

In the Holy Bible countless names are given to angels. Some are generic terms such as: Chosen Angels (1 Timothy 5:21); Hosts of Heaven (Luke 2:13); God's Heavenly Hosts (Psalm

103:21); and Sons of the Mighty (Psalm 29:1), while other names describe angels as 'messengers' and 'ministers' (Psalm 104:4). Also, when interpreting Nebuchadnezzar's dream, Daniel defined the angels as 'watchers' (Daniel 4:17, 23).

Two further groups, cherubim and seraphim dwelt around the throne of God and worshipped Him together, the seraphim hovering above the throne with the cherubim on either side of the throne.

Cherubim – Presence of God

The singular 'cherub' is mentioned in Genesis 3:24, Ezekiel 10:17–20, and 1 Kings 6:23–28. The word cherubim means to till or plough and is expressive of diligent service. They have four faces: one face is a cherub, the second a human being, the third a lion, and the fourth the face of an eagle. These are the same four living creatures John referred to in Revelation 4:7.

Guardians of the Throne

There are two types of cherubim both in form and function. The first group is of those who guard the Throne Room of God. They are in constant attendance upon the Lord, and are said to be guardians of light and the stars.

The second group of cherubim is also described as having perfect knowledge of God, surpassed only by the love of the seraphim who are mentioned thirty times as being 'the living creatures full of the life of God'.

Guardians of the Tree of Life

The second group was present when Adam and Eve were expelled from the Garden of Eden. God placed two cherubs on the east side of the garden as guardians to preserve the Tree of Life until, in the fullness of time, the redeemed ones will have the opportunity to enjoy the Garden of Eden once again. This promise is confirmed in Revelation 2:7:

> To those who are victorious, I will give them the right to eat from the Tree of Life, which is in the Paradise of God.

The cherubim played a major part in the worship of Yahweh in the tabernacle, representing the presence of God (Hebrew: Shekinah in their midst). At Moses' direction, two golden cherubs were fashioned then placed at each end of the Mercy Seat, with their heads down and their outstretched wings touching. Situated there, the cherubim stood for a new relationship between God and his people, with the laws placed inside, underpinning God's Presence and Holiness:

> There, above the cover between the two cherubim that are over the ark of the covenant law, I will meet with you and give you all my commands.
> *(Exodus 25:22)*

For as long as the Mercy Seat remained, the Israelites relied upon the Lord to lead them and save them from their enemies.

When the Mercy Seat disappeared, they then felt the glory of the Lord had departed.

Seraphim – Singers of Heaven

The seraphim, singular 'seraph' (translated from Hebrew: burning ones), are mentioned in Isaiah 6:1–7 and Revelation 4:8. These writers, though they lived hundreds of years apart, experienced a similar vision, describing the seraphim as having six wings each. According to Isaiah, two were used to cover their faces, two to cover their feet, and the last two were used to fly.

Brightest of the angelic orders, they glowed with the holy flame of divine love. Their job description was to serve as the caretakers of God's throne and to sing His praises.

It is thought by some that four seraphim sing the music of the spheres, regulating the movement of the heavens as it emanates from God. A bright light is said to flow from this, which makes it impossible for anyone to look upon them.

Work of the Angels

Fulfilment in a useful life on earth is an echo of the activities of the angels in heaven who were assigned specific jobs, according to a particular rank of angels or individual angels.

As stated, the seraphim and cherubim carried out their duties in God's presence, whilst other orders of the angelic host carried out their duties at His command on earth. Still other angels were given titles that specifically portray their occupations: messenger, healer, warrior, or protector.

All the angels, regardless of their position, were accountable to the Lord. This is confirmed in the book of Job, in a scene in the heaven of heavens. It speaks of the angels presenting themselves before the Lord, and recounting the many activities in which they had been involved. Lucifer was also present, seeking permission from God to test Job regarding his faith.

> Now there was a day when the sons of God came to present themselves before the Lord, and Satan came also among them.
> *(Job 1:6)*

Ministry of the Earthly Realm

Some people consider heaven as 'pie in the sky', unreal, or bearing no relevance to our existence and work here on earth. However, the Bible distinctly states that heaven will allow us mortals to experience fulfilment in this life and in the next. Humans are blessed in our life on earth to be filled not only with the Holy Spirit but also with a myriad of angels who are at our disposal to protect and guide us.

Messengers

The angels are heavenly emissaries sent by God to carry His message, offer help, or pronounce judgement. In the Old Testament, Moses is addressed by an angel from the burning bush (Exodus 3:1), and an angel wrestled with Jacob (Genesis 32:24). There are also twenty references of these beings in Judges as the *angels of the Lord*. In the New Testament, angels announced the birth of John, and announced the birth of Jesus to the Shepherds. It was also an angel who rolled back the stone and announced the resurrection of Jesus.

Protection

We are encouraged to read that although the Israelites are described in the King James Version, as a 'stiff necked' or 'stubborn' people, who were quick to complain, quick to turn to other idols, and quick to forget God's commandments, yet for all this, he never cast them off.

The promises he gave to Abraham, Isaac and Jacob are eternal:

> See I am sending an angel ahead of you to guard you along the way, and to bring you to the place I have prepared.
> *(Exodus 23:20–22)*

Like the Israelites, we can claim the many promises of the Lord, to those who trust in him for safety and protection, which are found throughout the Bible:

> No harm will overtake you; no disaster will come near your tent. For he will command his angels concerning you to guard you in all your ways.
> *(Psalm 91:10, 12)*

Guardian Angels of Children

Although the term 'Guardian Angel' does not appear in the Scriptures, this does not mean that these beings do not exist. Some believe there is one holy angel assigned to each child, while others believe the angels in general are responsible for all children. Matthew 18:10 supports this belief when he records that Jesus called a child to his side and then told all present to be converted and to humble themselves in a childlike manner. Jesus then continues to warn people to care for all children, with dire warnings to anyone who does not do this. Jesus concludes:

> See that you do not despise one of these little ones.
> For I tell you that their Angels in Heaven always see the
> face of my Father in heaven.
> *(Matthew 18:10)*

Similarly, another verse was recorded much earlier in history validating the respect of children. When Moses was preparing the people to enter the promised land under the new leadership of Joshua, he said:

> The little ones that you said would be taken captive,
> your children who do not yet know good from evil
> – they will enter the land.
> *(Deuteronomy 1:39)*

These references in scripture give a strong message to all believers to protect the young, as they are precious in God's sight.

Acknowledging Angels in Present-day Church Services

Even though they are not part of eternal salvation, angels are still recognised by many Christians in their lives and worship. The Nicene Creed, which has been an affirmation of our faith for centuries, is still recognised and sung in numerous churches. It begins with: 'We believe in one God, the Father, the Almighty, Maker of heaven and earth, of all that is seen and unseen' (Church of England in Australia, 1985).

Malcolm Godwin in his book *Angels: An Endangered Species* (1990) noted: 'the Angel is one of those Articles of Faith as unshaken as our belief in the existence of God'.

The recital of the Creed connects us with the activities of the seraphim as they continuously sing praises. When Isaiah describes this scene in his heavenly vision, he says he heard the heavenly choir, which was in the immediate presence of God. They were singing a glorious hymn that he noted was sung antiphonally with one group of angels echoing the other. A bright light is said to flow from this, which makes it impossible for anyone to look upon them. It was quite a fearsome sound causing the doorposts to shake:

> One cried one to another, and said, Holy, holy, holy is the Lord of hosts. All the earth is filled with His Glory.
> *(Isaiah 6:3)*

3. The Second Heaven

John had a similar vision:

> They did not rest day and night, saying, "Holy, holy, holy, Lord God Almighty. Who was, and is, and is to come? You are worthy, our Lord and God, to receive glory and honour and power, for You created all things."
> *(Revelation 4:8b, 11)*

This song of praise continues to resound throughout the world today. It is specifically important because of the use of the trisagion, the three-times Holy, which is a hymn to or an invocation to worship the thrice Holy One, God the Father, God the Son, and God the Holy Spirit.

Trisagion is a Hebrew method of triple repetition for emphasis. The use of the trisagion in the Bible is rare. One Biblical instance is found in Isaiah 6:3.

> They [the angels] were calling to one another: "Holy, holy, holy is the LORD Almighty; the whole earth is full of his glory."

Another trisagion in the book of Revelation is a severe warning prior to the sounding of the last three trumpets: *Woe, woe, woe, to the inhabitants, because of the last three trumpets* (Revelation 8:13).

There are, however, many instances of double repetitions, such as when Jesus said 'verily, verily, I say unto you'.

In the latter part of an Orthodox, Catholic, or Anglican

service, the whole congregation of worshippers from the communions repeats together:

> Therefore, with angels and archangels and with all the company of heaven we proclaim your great and glorious name, forever praising you and singing, Holy, holy, holy Lord God of power and might, heaven and earth are full of your glory. Hosanna in the highest (Church of England in Australia, 1985).

Hymns Based on this Acclamation of Faith

Countless hymns based on this trisagion have been sung by believers throughout history, even continuing to use them to proclaim their faith today. Some Christians believe that this triune message describes our triune God, and that when Christians on earth raise their voices to God, Sunday by Sunday, they become part of the heavenly choir worshipping together with the angels and those believers who have gone before. One of the greatest of these hymns, 'Holy, Holy, Holy, Lord God Almighty', is a paraphrase of Revelation 4:4–11.

The author of this majestic hymn, Reginald Heber (1783–1826), was born into an old, illustrious family. His father, a man of intellectual ability, was both fellow and tutor at Brasenose College, Oxford. Heber followed his father's footsteps and began a brilliant university career, but after travelling the world, accompanied by a friend, he returned to England and was ordained in the Church of England (Houghton, 1982).

Alfred Tennyson, as a poet laureate, thought the hymn to be fine, admiring its perfect spirituality and devotion, together with the purity of its language.

When the hymn was published in 1863, John Bacchus Dykes (1823–1876) wrote an accompanying tune called 'Nicea'. This is a significant name in the Christian church as it was at the Council of Nicea in 325 AD, when the church clearly enunciated its belief in the Trinity. The two final verses resound with an eternal affirmation!

HOLY, HOLY, HOLY! LORD GOD ALMIGHTY!

Holy, Holy, Holy! Lord God Almighty,
Early in the morning our song shall rise to Thee;
Holy, holy, holy, merciful and mighty!
God in three persons, blessed Trinity.

Holy, holy, holy! All the saints adore Thee,
Casting down their golden crowns around the glassy sea;
Cherubim and seraphim, falling down before Thee
Which wert and art and evermore shalt be.

Holy, holy, holy! Though the darkness hide thee.
Though the eye of sinful man Thy glory may not see,
only thou art holy; there is none beside thee,
perfect in pow'r, in love, and purity.

Holy, Holy, Holy! Lord God Almighty,
All Thy works shall praise thy name in earth and sky and sea.
Holy, Holy, Holy! Merciful and mighty
God in three persons, blessed Trinity.

Conclusion

It is an awe-inspiring thought that even now we are part of the Heavenly Host.

> Augustine had a strong sense that angels and men make up one city of God.

4. ARCHANGELS
Angels of His Presence

The celestial beings who rank highest in the company of angels are the archangels. The title archangel relates to the Hebrew faith and was possibly derived from the Greek words *arkhos* meaning chief, and *angelos* meaning heavenly messenger. There is no mention of these beings until the book of Daniel, when the archangels Michael and Gabriel appear. In considering the gifts given to each of the archangels and for what they are remembered, the Apocrypha needs to be included where the earliest references to a system of archangels, both singly and as a group, are found.

Although the books of the Apocrypha are not part of the Jewish canon, both the Jews and early church used their writings as a source of authority for various teachings that include angelology. Furthermore, the Dead Sea Scrolls (170 BC/68 AD/1956) and works by other groups like the Essenes have long been respected as a means of information on God's works during the intertestamental period.

The Apocrypha
Over the centuries Christians have differed as to the credibility of the Apocryphal writings which were written between 200 BC and 100 AD and are generally referred to as the intertestamental period. Many groups have often considered that there was silence

from God, together with no prominent prophets and teachers from Malachi to the birth of Christ. Like many Christians, I believe that God has never been without his witnesses.

Fortunately, this approach has changed greatly over the centuries. In 1534, Luther included the Apocrypha in his translation of the Bible, using the description 'intertestamental section', which name has been used from that time onwards. The preface to the Apocrypha in the Geneva Bible (GNV, 1560/2007) acknowledges:

> While these books were not received by a common consent to be read and expounded publicly in the church, nevertheless, as books proceeding from godly men they were received for the advancement and furtherance of the knowledge of history and for the instruction of good manners.

This period of history shows very clearly that God did not ignore His chosen people, as during this time there was a continuation of the development of the Jewish faith and knowledge of Himself. The writings of the Dead Sea Scrolls shed further light on the activities and struggles suffered by so many during this dark time.

In his book *Between the Testaments*, David Syme Russell (1976) writes :

> It has sometimes been suggested that the apocalyptic writings are simply imitative and that it is an attempt to

fulfil the word of scripture by means, which has no relation to the present because it arises out of literary reflection. But of the apocalyptic writers they were deeply religious men who believed that, like the prophets before them, their message was from God, and that they wrote under a divine compulsion.

Together with expressing personal faith, they also include visions of the coming of the Messiah, namely, the Son of Man, a title which Christ used when speaking of Himself.

During this tumultuous period of Jewish history, synagogue worship and education flourished together with the firm belief that they were God's chosen people. Furthermore, the writings of these men of faith described a graphical history of the battles in which the Jewish people were continually raging against their captors. These battles were fought just to be able to exist and keep their faith in God.

The Rabbis often considered that the names of the angels were brought back from Babylon by the returning exiles. In post-Biblical Judaism, and literature including the Apocrypha, some angels are named and given unique personalities, together with specific tasks. Several names from assorted groups are recorded. One such group names Gabriel, Michael, Uriel, Raguel, Remiel and Saraquel. These names are listed as representative of angelic beings who were leaders in God's kingdom.

Later, three of this group, together with Raphael, were given prominent roles to fulfil. They appear together in Enoch (Shaver, 1917/2015):

> Michael, Uriel, Raphael, and Gabriel looked down
> from heaven and saw much blood being shed on earth,
> and all the lawlessness being wrought upon the earth.
> *(1 Enoch 9:1)*

The Four Archangels

Gabriel, Michael, Uriel, and Raphael will be considered in depth as they appear in many circumstances throughout this chapter. Singly, these four archangels are found in different places. The first two, Gabriel and Michael, figure strongly in the Biblical text. References to the others are found in the apocryphal books: Uriel is named in Enoch and 2 Esdras, Raphael is mentioned in the Book of Tobit.

They called upon God when they saw the carnage on earth, then God sent them to destroy Azazel, who had corrupted humankind and caused Noah's flood. This story is found in Enoch Chapters 9 and 10. Chapter 10 concludes with a promise of God's eternal blessing and safety (Shaver, 1917/2015).

> All the children of men shall become righteous, and all
> nations shall offer adoration and shall praise Me,
> and all shall worship Me.
> *(1 Enoch 10:21)*

The evidence supplied in both the Apocrypha and Dead Sea Scrolls suggests that throughout this time many were encouraged to live their lives in accordance with God's holy laws and statutes regardless of the cost.

It can be noted that many thoughts and much language of the Dead Sea Scrolls have been duplicated in the New Testament. In the introduction of *The Scripture of the Dead Sea Sect* (170 BC/68 AD/1956):

- The members of the community considered themselves the elect of God, 'The brethren also affected the name of the elect.'
- 1 Peter: 1:1–2 commences his first epistle with "to God's elect scattered throughout the dispersion...who have been chosen according to the foreknowledge of God".
- The members wrote, 'The truth of God as revealed in Law 1 is constantly called the light.'
- John 1:7–9 writes, "there was a man named John, he came to bear witness to that Light".
- In the Book of Hymns section, the faithful regularly declared they stand in the eternal congregation of God and share the lot of the 'holy ones'.

In Ephesians 2:19, Paul writes, *"consequently you are no longer foreigners and strangers, but fellow citizens with God's people [the saints], and members of his household"*.

The similarity of faith, which motivated these Jewish groups and the early Christians, was seen when they both were prepared to die rather than deny God. (*The Scripture of the Dead Sea Sect*, 1956/170 BC/68 AD). Therefore, there is sufficient reliable evidence in the apocryphal writings to include certain archangels. Their very actions reinforce their place and position in God's mighty plan for the universe and the earth.

Angels of His Presence

In the *Talmud*, together with their ministries alluded to above, Michael, Gabriel, Raphael, and Uriel are considered the four angels of His presence who serve the *Shekinah*, which is the glory of the divine presence of God where He dwells.

The Jews believed that the angels who serve the Shekinah also head up the angelical system of angels, who are arranged in four groups before the Throne of God.

The term 'angel of His presence' first appeared in Isaiah, when Isaiah, as one of Israel's watchmen prayed a penitential confession and prayer for Israel's restoration. The prayer appraises God's passionate act towards His people, despite their unfaithfulness to him:

> In all their distress he too was distressed, and the
> Angel of His Presence saved them.
> *(Isaiah 63:9)*

This term is also used in the New Testament by Gabriel when he visited Zachariah and announced the birth of John. The angel said to him,

> I am Gabriel. I stand in the presence of God, and I have
> been sent to speak to you and tell you the good news.
> *(Luke 1:19)*

There is a description of the angels of the presence found in *The Scripture of the Dead Sea Sect* (170 BC/68 AD/1956) under the heading 'Book of Hymns' Part II: Praise to God. This passage describes their work in the highest heavens:

> All these men hast Thou brought into communion with Thee, and hast given them common estate with the angels of Thy Presence. There stands no intermediary among them to approach Thee on their behalf, for they themselves are answered from out of Thy glorious mouth. They are Thy courtiers, sharing the high estate of the heavenly beings.

This, intermingling with the angels and the elect ones, is described in Revelation:

> All the angels were standing around the throne and around the elders, and the four living creatures. They fell down on the faces before the throne and worshipped God, saying: "Amen! Praise and glory and wisdom and thanks and honour and power and strength be to our God for ever and ever. Amen!"
> *(Revelation 7:11–12)*

Uriel – Fire/light of God

Together with the highest position of angel of presence:

> Uriel is over the world (Paradise) and over Tartarus (Hell).
> (Enoch 20:1)

Another of Uriel's activities appears to be one of instruction to humans. This ministry is portrayed in both Enoch and 2 Esdras. Uriel was sent as a guide, and to interpret the series of questions Ezra had about the corruption of humankind:

> The angel that had been sent to me, whose name was Uriel, answered and said to me ... I have been sent to show you the three ways and put before you three problems.
> (2 Esdras 4:1,3)

He also acted as a guide for Enoch when he sought enlightenment to know and understand the way:

> In those days the angel Uriel answered and said to me: Behold, I have shown thee everything, Enoch, and I have revealed everything to thee that thou shouldst see this sun.
> (Enoch 80:1)

The Anglicans and Eastern Orthodox Church consider Uriel as patron of the arts, including music and poetry and high sciences; they also recognise his ability to inspire and awaken the intellect . He is often depicted carrying a book, or a papyrus scroll, standing for wisdom.

Raphael – God Who Heals

Raphael is another archangel of the post-exilic Rabbinic tradition, as well as of certain Christian traditions. He appears to have been given power and authority to act on behalf of the Eternal God.

> Raphael, one of the holy ones, who are over the spirits of men.
>
> (Enoch 20:2)

He, with Uriel, explained the meaning of the visions Enoch was experiencing.

> Then Raphael answered, one of the holy angels who was with me, and said unto me, "These hollow places have been created for this very purpose ... that the spirits of the children of men should assemble here."
>
> (Enoch 22:3)

Another of his unique giftedness was healing, as his name implies Jehovah Rapha (God who heals). Enoch writes:

> The second, who is set over all the diseases, and all the wounds of the children of men, is Raphael.
>
> (Enoch 40:12)

In this role, he played a major part in the book of Tobit.

It is a story about the lives of two people who have been beset by misfortune. The main characters in this tale are a righteous Jew named Tobit, who had become blind, and Sarah, the daughter of Raguel, who was possessed by a demon. Both these people turned to God in distress. God heard their prayers and sent the archangel Raphael to heal them (Tobit 3:16–17).

Although Raphael is not in mentioned the Bible, some

branches of Christianity believe he is associated with the unnamed angel mentioned in John (5:4), who stirred the water at the healing pool of Bethsaida.

In the Catholic church today he is the patron of travellers, nurses, physicians, medical workers and the blind. As a patron of those people who dedicate their lives to healing the sick, he is an angel whom all Christians can respect.

Gabriel – God's Hero or Messenger and Comforter

The archangel Gabriel is mentioned by name four times in the Scriptures: twice in Daniel, and twice in Luke. Although unmentioned by name, it is thought that he may have been the angel who spoke with Daniel a third time in (Daniel 10), where he was working with Michael, one of the chief princes.

> While I, Daniel, was watching the vision and trying to understand it, there before, stood one who looked like a man. And I heard a man's voice from the Ulai calling, Gabriel, tell this man the meaning of the vision.
> *(Daniel 8:16)*

Gabriel went on to explain forthcoming events that would take place in the world's history. Later, in the first year of Darius, when Daniel perceived that the end of the years of exile for the Jews was approaching, he began to pray, confessing his own sins and the sins of God's people. The actual prayer was made up of lengthy supplications, together with fasting and sackcloth and ashes (Daniel 9:3). Whilst Daniel was thus praying, Gabriel visited him once again:

> While I was still in prayer, Gabriel, the man I had seen in the earlier vision, came to me in swift flight about the time of the evening sacrifice. He instructed me and said to me, "Daniel, I have now come to give you, insight and understanding – for you are highly esteemed."
> *(Daniel 9:21, 23)*

This encouraging word was spoken to a man of God, who was wrestling with so many issues which appeared to overwhelm him. Not only was Daniel stressed at this but those Jews with him in exile faced a similar situation. Hence God showed his enduring love and care for them through these comforting words to Daniel.

A third vision was revealed to Daniel in Chapter 10. This whole chapter is concerned with Daniel's preparation for this event. During this time Daniel was mourning in sackcloth and ashes, neither eating nor drinking, for three weeks.

When Daniel had no strength left, he saw a vision of a heavenly being. Later, when lying down in a deep sleep, he heard his words: *'Here a hand touched me, and sent me trembling, on my hands and knees'* (Daniel 10:10). It appeared to be Gabriel who touched him, as he had interpreted other revelations to Daniel.

The one who looked like a man continued, asking Daniel not to be afraid as he had heard Daniel's words on the first day when they were uttered. He explained how the prince of the

Persian kingdom resisted him for three weeks, then Michael came to help him.

In the final two verses, the angel tells of an ongoing war that is raging throughout the universe between the forces of good and evil, between God and Satan.

> So, he said, "Do you know why I have come to you? Soon I will return to fight against the prince of Persia, and when I go, the prince of Greece will come, but first let me tell you what is written in the Book of Truth. No one supports me against them except Michael, your prince."
> *(Daniel 10:20)*

In the New Testament, Gabriel continues to bring joy and hope to the world, as he is given the amazing task of proclaiming the imminent birth of Christ. He first appeared to Zachariah as he administered his priestly duties during his allotted course in the Temple.

> Then an angel of the Lord appeared to him, standing at the right side of the altar of incense. But the angel said unto him. "Do not be afraid, Zachariah: your prayer has been heard. Your wife Elizabeth will bear you a son, and you are to call him John."
> *(Luke 1:11, 13)*

Later he revealed himself to Zachariah and Elizabeth: *I am Gabriel. I stand in the presence of God* (Luke 1:19), and again, reminded them that they were going to produce a son, who would prepare the way for the Messiah. The angel Gabriel then revealed himself to Mary saying:

> In the sixth month of Elizabeth's pregnancy, God sent the angel Gabriel to Nazareth, a town in Galilee ... The virgin's name was Mary. The angel went to her and said, "Greetings, you who are highly favoured! The Lord is with you."
> *(Luke 1:26–29)*

Michael – Who is Like Unto God? Who is Equal to God?

Michael is a Hebrew word recorded as a name of an archangel in the Book of Daniel. He is the first angel thus named. He is also spoken of as the great prince, mighty warrior, and leader of the people. He held two positions! The first was to be warrior and protector of Israel.

> At that time Michael, the great prince who protects your people, the nation of Israel, and the Jewish people will arise.
> *(Daniel 12:1)*

Angels are part of many a scene throughout scripture, and Gabriel and Michael play an important role in the book of Daniel. When Daniel was weakened by fasting and emotionally distressed by the presence of an angel, Gabriel encouraged him, then explained his delay in coming to his aid. He was accosted by the evil Persian Empire as well as being busy fighting the evil ones with only Michael to help him (Daniel 10:10,11:21).

The second position he held was leader of the heavenly hosts. Revelation 12:7–10 describes a war in heaven between angels led by the archangel Michael against those led by 'the dragon', identified by some as the devil or Satan.

Frederick Holweck wrote in the *Catholic Encyclopedia* (1911) an article named 'Michael the Archangel':

> St. John speaks of the great conflict at the end of time, which also reflects the ongoing battle at the beginning of time. He added that Michael's name was the war-cry of the good angels in the battle fought in heaven against the enemy and his followers.

Michael is also named in the book of Jude where it is said that he contended with the devil over the body of Moses. Jude is referring to the burial of Moses, which was situated in an unknown place where Satan could not use his body for any nefarious activity.

> The archangel Michael, when he was disputing with
> the devil about the body of Moses, did not himself
> dare to condemn him for slander but said,
> "The Lord rebuke you ".
> (Jude 1:9)

Thus, we can note how the angels in heaven were given tasks, together with the ability to successfully fulfil their duties. This is very encouraging to all people on earth, helping us to understand our innate need to work. Just like the angels, we have received a diversity of gifts from God which have been expanded throughout our time on earth. They include all those gifts which are in heaven itself – sciences, mathematical equations, medical research, architecture, music, literature, and the arts.

Primary Task

The primary task of these archangels was to guard the Holy One on His throne of righteousness. They, with the myriad of angels (which includes the cherubim and seraphim), delighted in continually glorifying and praising the Holy Lord. Enoch affirms that:

> They stand before Thy Glory and bless, praise, and extol, saying: Holy, holy, holy, is the Lord of Spirits that filleth the earth with spirit.
> (Enoch 29:9)

As seen earlier, the song they sang was taken up by John, in Revelation, and Christians have continued to make it resound throughout the ages. An early hymn concludes our celebration of the angelic host and their contribution to our present praise and glory of eternal God.

A beautiful hymn describing the work of the archangels

was composed by St Joseph the hymnographer, who was born in Sicily in 816 AD, son of Christian parents – Plotinus and Agatha.

Because of Arab incursions into Sicily in 830 AD, he moved with his family to Greece. Later, he became a monk of the Orthodox Church at the Monastery of Patmos. He is credited with composing about one thousand hymns, many of which are still used in the liturgy of the Orthodox Church (Venerable St Joseph the Hymnographer, 2022).

It is encouraging to recognise that this hymn includes the worship and work of the angels as portrayed in the Bible. Knowing the truths about angels and their position in God's eternal scheme is unchangeable. These early Christians, like Daniel of old, acknowledged that the angels are part of our lives on earth.

The hymn 'Stars of the Morning, So Gloriously Bright' was translated into English by John Mason Neale in 1862, composed by Henry Thomas Smart in 1868, and is a trisagion.

STARS OF THE MORNING, SO GLORIOUSLY BRIGHT

Stars of the morning, so gloriously bright,
Filled with celestial splendour and light,
These that, where night ever followeth the day,
Raise the trisagion ever and aye.

These are thy ministers, these dost thou own
Lord God of Sabaoth, nearest thy throne.
These are thy messengers, these dost thou send
Help of the helpless ones! man to defend .

"Who, like the Lord?" thunders Michael the chief;
Raphael, "the cure of God", comforted grief.
And as at Nazareth, prophet of peace;
Gabriel, "the light of God", bringeth release.

Then, when the earth was first poised in mid space;
Then, when the planets first sped on their race.
Then, where were ended the six days' employ;
Then all the sons of God shouted for joy.

Still let them succour us, still let them fight;
Lord of angelic hosts, battling for right;
Till, where their anthems they ceaselessly pour,
We with the angels may bow and adore.

Conclusion

A touching scene is set before us which describes Jewish children as they repeat their nightly devotions. At the end of the Bedtime Shema, a collection of liturgical texts was recited before going to sleep. They were prayers asking God to 'protect and guard our souls'. The text names the archangels cited above:

Michael, to my right side and Gabriel to my left, before me Uriel, and behind me Raphael, and over my head God's Shekinah (The presence of God).

5. LUCIFER

His Glorious Creation

Lucifer, also known as Satan and the devil, is the third archangel mentioned in the Bible. He is referred to in seven books of the Old Testament and every writer of the New Testament includes references to him and his deeds. He first appeared in the Garden of Eden where he tempted Adam and Eve. He has been tempting humans from that time on (Lockyer, 1995).

In describing Satan and his attributes before the fall, I will direct my remarks to the name Lucifer. Lucifer was first used in *The Latin Vulgate Bible* (382 AD/2012) and was a generic Latin term meaning Venus as 'the Morning Star'. Later it appeared in the King James Version of the Holy Bible.

> How art thou fallen from heaven,
> O Lucifer, son of the morning!
> *(Isaiah 14:12)*

Not only did God make Lucifer a superior being, greater than all the other inhabitants of the heavens, he endowed him with a greater personality and intelligence, and gave him a free will.

Theologians have differed as to whether Isaiah and Ezekiel are referring to the kings of Babylon and Tyre, or Satan. The verses appear to be similar to Daniel's visions in which two references are filled with symbolism. The names apparently having double meanings: that of Satan and his fall, together with future events.

Ezekiel 28:11–19 is dualistic in its meaning. On the one hand it is predicting the eventual destruction of Tyre, which did not come to pass until Alexander the Great built a causeway to the Island and captured it. On the other hand, there are many descriptors here in Ezekiel which point to heavenly ideas . Ezekiel gives us a vivid portrayal of Lucifer, describing how he was the embodiment of all the perfection of God's creation. This is what the Sovereign Lord says:

> You were the seal of perfection, full of wisdom and perfect in beauty. You were in Eden, the garden of God; every precious stone adorned you: carnelian, chrysolite and emerald, topaz, onyx and jasper, lapis lazuli, turquoise and beryl. Your settings and mountings were made of gold; on the day you were created they were prepared.
> *(Ezekiel 28:12–13)*

Lucifer was entrusted with many roles which included chief cherub, guarding the throne, bearer of light, star of the morning and chief musician. In his role as Guardian Cherub he protected God's holiness:

> You were anointed as guardian cherub, for I ordained you there on the holy mount of God. You walked among the fiery stones. You were blameless in all your ways from the day you were created till wickedness was found in you.
> *(Ezekiel 28:14–15)*

Lucifer's Garments – Lucifer was Dressed Suitably for his High Position:

> You were in Eden, the garden of God; every precious stone adorned you. Carnelian, chrysolite and emerald, topaz, onyx and jasper, lapis lazuli, turquoise and beryl. Your settings and mountings were made of gold, on the day you were created they were prepared.
> *(Ezekiel 28:13)*

Lucifer was decked with dazzling stones, resembling a display of costly jewels even today. His apparel revealed his role in heaven. This records the second time these stones are mentioned in the Bible.

The first occurred after the Holy Place in the desert had been set up. God chose the High Priest of the tribe of Levi as his earthly representative and clothed him accordingly. His garments included a breastplate containing twelve precious stones set in gold, signifying the twelve tribes of Israel, and showing the grace and mercy of God.

Lucifer was clothed in these garments, which were suitable to his position as Guardian of God.

Of the twelve precious stones which adorned the High Priest's breastplate, nine of these precious stones were set in finest gold and placed on Lucifer's garments; the three stones absent on Lucifer's garments were amethyst, ligure and agate.

It is both significant and interesting that the apparel which was used by Lucifer was so like the priestly garments which God designed for his earthly representatives, which were firstly to be used in the tabernacle, then in the more permanent dwelling, the temple. The similarity to the garments of Lucifer appears to suggest God expected his priests on earth to dress to a remarkably high and beautiful standard as was shown in his Holy Throne Room.

Lucifer, the Chief Musician

Before his fall, Lucifer was best known for his musical talents – resulting in his name becoming synonymous with all musical activity. Although Lucifer was anointed for the post of Music Director, he was not alone in this heavenly ministry; God's created angels aided him. Their job was to present continual praise and worship throughout the night and day.

He was very well-equipped for the task! Not only was he the embodiment of all the wonderful attributes mentioned above, but he was also given extraordinary musical gifts. These gifts were exemplified in the fact that he not only had great talent, but the means to express them were built into him during his creation.

In his book *Your Adversary the Devil* (1997), Dr J. Dwight Pentecost writes:

> Musical instruments were originally designed to be a means of praising and worshipping God. It was not necessary for Lucifer to learn to play a musical instrument. He had a built-in pipe organ, or he was an organ. Glorious music emanated from within Lucifer's own body, music which would have taken one human being many hours to master and a whole lifetime of study hours to compose. Also, it would take the same amount, if not more time to practice, to achieve a shadow of this expression of wondrous sound. Lucifer did not have to look for someone to play the organ so that he could sing the doxology – He was the doxology!

Primaeval Music

When I first began researching the creative arts with emphasis upon my own discipline – music – I always considered that it began in Genesis where Jubal is named the father of all who play stringed instruments and pipes (Genesis 4:21).

Jubal may have been the father of these instrumentalists, but this prompted the question: Were the gifts of music and rhythm developed in Genesis, or were they part of the eternal praise which has resonated throughout the whole of the universe from eternity to eternity?

After much study and consideration, I believe the answer to this question is yes, they were part of the universe prior to the creation. During the course of these studies, it will be understood that from eternity to eternity, music and rhythm are part of the heavens, as well as part of the creative process. Lucifer is shown to have had all the equipment for eternal praise to the Almighty.

The Human Voice – Lucifer's Equipment

The human voice can be considered the first musical instrument, as it is the oldest and most natural sound source from which music can consciously be made. The essential factor in producing sound is motion, which arises from a vibratory body, generating waves of density in the air. The human voice works on the same principles.

During the eighteenth century, the term 'vocal cord' was introduced when it was thought they might function like strings of other musical instruments. These folds react to the pressure from the breath meeting and vibrating and changing length as the pitch is raised or lowered (Karoly, 1981). These voices are used to described both compass and colour tone, and usually encompasses just over two octaves, although both ends may be extended in length by trained singers.

The great Biblical entities who were privileged to enter the Holy Place recognised the sounds of singing together with the instruments the elders were playing:

> He went and took the scroll from the right hand of him who sat on the throne. And when he had taken it, the four living creatures and the twenty-four elders fell down before the lamb. Each one had a harp, and

they were holding golden bowls of incense, which are the prayers of God's people. And they sang a new song, saying: "You are worthy to take the scroll and to open its seals."

(Revelation 5:7–9)

The voice can be considered the very first musical instrument and is the only one, like with Lucifer, which is part of the performer. Therefore, it stands to reason that Adam and Eve were familiar with these heavenly sounds and repeated what they heard to their offspring. From this beginning, many humans would have experimented with their own voices and sought to create instruments out of the suitable material available at the time.

Singing is not the only use made of the voice, the art of speech was equally important as communication is a necessary part of the human equipment in countless ways, including survival. Speech made it possible from the beginning for people to interact with each other in their daily activities.

From birth, babies make certain vocalisations to express hunger, alarm, and fear in the face of danger. Later, they learn how to communicate orally with those around them. From the reference to the Tower of Babel, all the people of earth originally spoke the same language. As the Bible recounts, when they became so wicked and turned against God, he confused their language, making it impossible for them to understand one another.

> But the Lord came down to see the city and the tower which the people were building. The Lord said, "If as one people speaking the same language, they have begun to do this, then nothing they plan to do will be impossible for them. Come, let us go down and confuse their language so they will not understand each other."
> *(Genesis 11:6–7)*

From the earliest time, speech also enabled human beings to be in fellowship with their Creator, as seen in Genesis, where Adam and Eve walked and talked with God in the Garden of Eden.

> Then the man and his wife heard the sound of the Lord God, as He was walking in the garden in the cool of the day and they hid from the Lord God among the trees of the garden.
> *(Genesis 3:8–10)*

This gift of human speech was not given to any other animal, although, when interacting with their own kind, each species, have a unique form of communication.

Most humans can sing unless they have certain disabilities. One such disability is deafness, making it impossible for anyone to hear sounds orally and then reproduce what they hear without assistance.

Music and singing were woven into the fabric of everyday life, from the poorest of the land to the mighty palaces of kings. All could indulge in making instruments from the most primitive resources to the most sophisticated.

Singing with instruments has been used throughout the ages to express praises to God or false gods. Songs of victory escorted the soldiers as they returned triumphant from battle. Joyous singing and dancing was performed at celebrations such as harvest times, weddings and there were even dirges of lament to be sung at funerals.

Intonation – Pitch

In earlier times a Precentor/Leader intoned the first line or phrase of a plainsong melody, to give the pitch or tone of the tune that followed. The singers would then repeat or imitate this orally. This could possibly have been one form of ancient singing which came into the Christian church through the Jews.

Although historically one is unable to state what early music sounded like, musicians like Yehudi Menuhin (1979), after studying ancient groups of people who are still extant in modern times, consider that pitch may have developed out of the natural inflections in the language used. These nuances may have caused impassioned speech to become chanting and chanting to become singing.

From the creation story this appears unlikely, as Adam and Eve were created with their vocal mechanism intact, as they spoke to the Lord in the Garden. Also, it would appear that they would have heard the angel's songs of praise, then imitated what they heard around them.

Menuhin is correct in saying that humans would have

used, and still do use natural inflections in language, as seen when emotions change, causing a person to react by raising or lowering the voice. Many of today's languages are called tonal, which means when two words are spoken in different pitches they often have entirely different meanings.

From time immemorial, intoned speech (chanting) has been part of the language of worship. It continues to be used in many religious cultures, including Christianity and Judaism, as a means of elevating words and ideas uttered to a more spiritual level.

Voices are naturally tuned into four different categories:

- Soprano
- Alto
- Tenor
- Bass.

With this natural division of the human voice, it seems logical that those of ancient times would have experimented with these sounds, although from our point of view it is impossible to judge due to lack of any evidence. The ability to record sounds was a much later invention.

Vocal music together with instrumental music are freely given to all regardless of country, nationality, religion, or politics. Wherever one travels throughout the world today, it is likely that delightful singing, together with all kinds of musical instruments, will be heard.

Conclusion

Biblical evidence appears to confirm that music and sound was not created by human endeavour but were a continuation of the musical sounds and rhythms throughout the heavens above.

The writer of Ecclesiastes understood this concept when he wrote:

> What has been will be again, what has been done will be done again. There is nothing new under the sun.
> *(Ecclesiastes 1:9)*

This thought was taken up by Yehudi Menuhin (1979), when he wrote:

> Man invents nothing. For the most part he discovers, drawing on the experience of the world outside, instruments, and within himself.

6. LUCIFER'S EQUIPMENT

Tuning

Although speech can express so many ideas in so many ways, the singing voice enables the singer to convey ideas more thoughtfully and passionately.

The human voice is the sound source and tuning of all musical instruments developed throughout the ages. From this source, musical instruments are all tuned to the same pitches, regardless of what scale is used.

William Zeitler (2022) records that there are 1490 possible musical scales based on the standard Western/European chromatic form. These include the major and minor scales, modes (which are scales commonly used by the Greeks and other ancient civilisations), and the micro scales which remain in India.

Isaiah and Ezekiel together describe the instruments which Lucifer used in his worship of the Lord which then became part of his downfall.

> All your pomp has been brought down to the grave,
> along with the noise of your harps.
> *(Isaiah 14:11)*

> The workmanship of your timbrels [timbrels] and pipes
> was prepared for you on the day you were created.
> *(Ezekiel 28:13 NKJV)*

Instrumental sounds were divided into pipes, harps and tabrets, which have stood for music of all kinds and have been in existence since the earliest times. Wherever there has been human habitation, archaeologists have found countless drawings of singers with or without instruments, displayed in ancient cities and walls of buildings, together with ancient relics in caves and graves.

I came across a similar idea written in 1879 by the renowned music educator of the time John Stainer (2018). He wrote, "I do not intend to list every instrument in the Bible but will include a few to demonstrate the relationship between those earlier instruments and those still in use today."

Although the true origins of most instruments are unknown, many of our modern instruments appear to have been in existence alongside humanity, albeit in their primitive form. Most are over four thousand years old and appear to have come from the Mediterranean area, spreading into Syria, Persia and Egypt. As the Bible records, Jubal, a couple of generations later than Adam, began making and playing early instruments.

> His brother's name was Jubal; he was the father of all
> who play stringed instruments and pipe.
> *(Genesis 4:21)*

Throughout the Old Testament, strings and pipes, together with other instruments, continued to play an important role in Israel, as well as in other early civilisations.

Ancient Stringed Instruments

Generally, stringed instruments had two supports, leaving the third free to vibrate. Three things that make strings produce different notes are tension, thickness, and length. The shorter, thinner, and tighter the strings, the higher the notes.

These strings made little noise on their own, so they needed some kind of sounding board to amplify the vibrations. This amplification occurred after the strings were struck, when the sound of the note continued to resonate via the sound box.

Two ancient stringed instruments were popular during Biblical times, the first being the kinnor, usually translated as the lyre, the second was the nebel or nevel, sometimes called harp or psaltery.

Kinnor – Kithara – Lyre

The kinnor/kithara is one of the most noteworthy instruments of the Jewish people. It was possibly a simple lyre or harp. It is mentioned forty-two times in the Bible. It usually had somewhere between six and ten strings.

David used a ten-stringed instrument in many of his psalms. The kinnor became the major instrument of the nation of Israel in Palestine, continuing in popularity during the Jewish monarchy from King David onwards. It was also used in the

Old Testament during family celebrations, religious praise, and for therapeutic occasions – like when David played to Saul to relieve his depression (1 Samuel 16:16).

Nebel – sometimes called harp or psaltery

The other stringed instrument was the nebel, meaning 'skin bottle', or jar, which may suggest a swollen soundbox like a lyre or lute; although in later times it was thought the instrument may have developed into something like a guitar with a longer neck. It is mentioned twenty-eight times in the Old Testament.

A number of other well-constructed lyres have been found; the one found at Ur had twelve strings. The nebel had three sides, the lower being a box-like structure, possibly the sound box. The other two sides consisted of a wooden frame; the third being formed by the longest strings. The instrument was held under an arm or rested on a shoulder.

Both the kinnor and nebel were made of fir wood, and later, almug (which John Stainer thought to be a red sandalwood of India). These were not only used as solo instruments, but on some occasions they were used together with other instruments. David was skilled on both these instruments!

Josephus gives some idea as to the difference between a kinnor and nebel by writing that the kinnor, with six to ten strings, was plucked with a plectrum held between the first finger and thumb. The plectrum may have been a small staff or a piece of quill, made of bone or ivory. The nebel, however, was a twelve-stringed instrument and was played with the fingers.

When Samuel ordained Saul as the first King over Israel,

the prophets celebrated the occasion by singing and playing instruments, which included the nebel. On another happy occasion, the strings were used to celebrate the return of the Ark of the Covenant from Kiriath-Jearim, where they prepared a tent in Jerusalem.

David told the leaders of the Levites to appoint their fellow Levites as musicians, to make a joyful sound with musical instruments: lyres, harps, and cymbals.

Later, David gave further instructions to the musicians, appointing some to sound the bronze cymbals, and others to play the nebels (harps), according to Alamoth, whilst others were instructed to play the lyres (kinnors) according to Sheminith. Alamoth and Sheminith are presumed to be two of many instructions given as to how musicians would interpret their performances.

Finally, the head Levite oversaw the singing together with the trumpets. What a glorious occasion!

Guitar

There are a number of early instruments considered to be the precursors of the guitar, the instrument which has become iconic in our modern society. One such supposition is that it originated in Mesopotamia, and was considered to be a member of the tanbur family.

Tanbur is a word to describe various long-necked instruments with plucked strings. Distinguishing features of the guitar that set it apart from other members of the tanbur family are its long-fretted neck, a flat wooden soundboard, ribs, and a flat back, often with incurved sides.

Some say it originated from an early form of the Persian Arabic lute. This instrument was half pear-shaped in appearance and is thought to pre-date the guitar. It is believed that the lute was brought to Western Europe by Crusaders returning from the Middle East.

Stringed Instruments Today

Although there are countless stringed instruments today, and mostly all look alike, there are three main groups or families.

The first is the violin family, which includes violins, violas, cellos and basses. The second is the harp family which includes the harp, lyre and zither. And the third is the guitar family which includes guitar, lute, mandolin and banjo.

Each group works on the same principles as ancient instruments, as all three families use some type of wooden box for vibrations, with strings stretched across it in some way.

Ancient Wind Instruments

Ancient pipes – there were two types of pipes in ancient times:
- khalil or halil which were possibly reed instruments
- machol or flute/flue pipe.

Khalil/Halil – Reed Instruments

Many people, including John Stainer, believe that the first woodwind instrument named in the Bible is the khalil/halil.

The khalil seems to have been an oboe- or clarinet-like instrument, made of reed or bone. Some musicologists believe possibly the khalil included double pipes. These, together with double-reed instruments, were common wind instruments of the ancient Near East.

The khalil appears in the Old Testament in connection with celebrations and following a military victory. Later, it was also linked with prophetic ecstasy.

Machol / Flute / Flue pipe is also grouped into two types – vertical and transverse

The vertical flutes, which may have been like an old Egyptian oblique-made pipe, made a sound by blowing into the open end of the tube.

As today, the transverse flutes with closed end were played by blowing across a hole pierced in the side. Ancient Egyptian relics show a reed-flute, held obliquely and blown across the upper open end. Other specimens shown in ancient sculptures and frescos have been of various lengths.

Aulos

Later, the aulos of the Greeks, and then the tibia of the Romans, were described as having a single or double-reeded pipe, similar to the khalil of earlier times. These accounts appear to include two important divisions of modern instruments – clarinet and oboe. Archaeologists working in Israel have found many such pipes dating to Roman times (Dowley, 2011). They were thought to be used at weddings and wakes (Matthew 9:23; 11:17).

Ancient Egyptian relics show a reed-flute (oboe) held obliquely and blown across the upper open end. Other specimens shown in ancient sculptures and frescos have been of various lengths

In early times players often carried 'tongue boxes' to carry their tongues or reeds separately, as do modern players of oboes and clarinet even today.

Shofar

The most iconic instrument in Israel's history that is still used today is the shofar geren or keren, meaning shrill sound. The shofar is the most frequently mentioned in the Hebrew Scriptures – some seventy-four times; playing an important part in the development of Israel's worship.

In its primitive form it was constructed out of the horn – often called 'jobel-horn' sometimes translated as 'ram's horn', which is thought to be the source of the word 'jubilee'.

The shofar is unique among the instruments of ancient Israel as it can be played as a solo instrument. It is capable of sounding two or three tones – a 'voice', a 'trumpet blast' a 'shout' and even a 'moaning'. These sounds would have been used to make different signals in religious or military situations.

It was the very loud sound of the shofar that the Israelites heard from the thick cloud together with great thunders and lightnings rolled round the holy mount, causing everyone to tremble with fear.

> On the third day there was thunder and lightning, with a thick cloud over the mountain, and a very loud trumpet blast. Everyone in the camp trembled.
> *(Exodus 19:16)*

Another important occasion when the shofar with the silver trumpets was sounded occurred on the first day of the seventh month, to announce the third major festival of the year, seven days before Yom Kippur (the annual Jewish Day of Atonement fast).

The Lord said to Moses:

> On the first day of the seventh month, you are to have a day of Sabbath rest, a sacred assembly commemorated with trumpet blasts. It is a day for you to sound the trumpets.
> *(Leviticus 23:23)*

Wind Instruments Today

These instruments are not always made solely of wood, but include a whole range of other materials including horn, bone, ivory and plastic. Not only are they made of many materials, but they also make more different sounds than any other family of instruments.

As with the ancient instruments, the noise made by a wind instrument comes from the air inside its pipe vibrating regularly. All tube-instruments can only give a series of sounds called natural harmonics or overtones, which are produced by gradually increasing the pressure of air from the column through the lips.

Other woodwind instruments are divided into groups, according to the way their air column is made to vibrate. Many, like the clarinet, include a single reed fastened by a ligature to a mouthpiece held between the player's lips, causing it to vibrate. The oboe has a double reed which is gripped between the lips through which the wind is blown.

The shofar, the father of the horn, has been used as a hunting horn, and from there, with much ingenuity and development, became the double-horn, much enjoyed for its smooth sound. Today, the modern horns are used in bands and orchestras.

Ancient Brass Instruments

Silver Trumpets – Hazozra/Chatsostserah

Similar to the woodwind instruments, the sound of brass instruments is made by the vibration of the air column within the instruments. In ancient times there were many types of brass instruments, using different methods to produce sound.

Moses was commanded to make two silver trumpets, which were blown by the priests.

Josephus (37–38/1987) states that these silver or metal trumpets were about 1.5 metres in length and were fashioned long, straight, and slender with a wide mouth (Numbers 10:1–10).

They were used to gather the people together. When one silver trumpet was blown, the heads of the tribes assembled, to be consulted about matters of the community. When two were blown, it was a signal for all the people to gather at the tabernacle.

These trumpets were also in the tabernacle as part of its sacred activities, which included bringing their sacrifices to the altar, as well as Sabbaths and festival days. On the 'Feast of Trumpets' they were played with the shofars.

Archaeologists have discovered countless hieroglyphics of early brass instruments, on ancient monuments and other buildings.

Brass Instruments Today

Today, brass instruments include the trumpet, trombone, tuba, horn, fugal-horn, cornet, and later saxophone, to name a few.

Silver trumpets have always been associated with times of ritual connected with royalty or church dignities.

Ancient Percussion Instruments

All the nations during Biblical times appear to have had drums of various kinds, and because they were portable, they were comparatively small. Some from Egypt consisted of a wood or copper cylinder covered with parchment at both ends.

These two heads were beaten with hands and were used as accompaniments to the singing and dancing.

Tabrets – Toph

The ancient instrument known in Hebrew as the toph is a type of hand drum with a circular wooden frame and a membrane skin, like a tambourine without the metal jingles (Dowley, 2011).

It is mentioned sixteen times in the Old Testament, often being played by women. Sometimes they were used as a solo instrument.

The toph is first referenced when Laban rebuked Jacob for having stealthily left him, instead of departing in an honourable way accompanied with songs, toph and kinnor (Genesis 31:27 KJV).

It also appeared as a timbrel after Hebrews escaped from Egypt.

> Miriam, the prophetess, the sister of Aaron, took a timbrel in her hand; and all the women went out after her with timbrels and with dances.
> *(Exodus 15:20)*

The toff does not appear to have been featured in temple music.

Kettledrums

John Stainer (1879), considered this instrument a prototype of our modern kettledrum, being formed by stretching parchment over the open end of a basin of metal or earthenware. It was used by the Egyptians, and at first it was small and easily carried by a handle.

From this beginning, it grew to about a metre, which later was replaced by three feet; the bowl became more rounded which resulted with freer vibration.

Cymbals

The word cymbal is from a root meaning to tingle or tinkle (Lockyer, 2004). These instruments ranged in size and style starting with small cymbal-shaped metal instruments called crotales, which often gave a note of an actual pitch.

A popular cymbal appears to have been an instrument consisting of a circular, coned, or flat metal plate that can be struck with a mallet or used as a pair and struck together. Two types of cymbals are described in Psalm 150:5 KJV, *Praise Him upon loud cymbals; praise Him with high sounding cymbals.*

Another cymbal common in early times is the finger cymbal worn on the hands and often fixed to the thumb and forefinger. They are still popular in many countries and called castanets. It appears that the use of cymbals in the Bible was confined to religious ceremonies and not used for dancing. They are mentioned when the ark was being returned from Kirjath-jearim (1 Chronicles 15:12), and at the dedication of Solomon's Temple (2 Chronicles 29:2).

Systrums

Numbers 10:1–10 describes another noisemaking instrument – the systrum which means to 'shake'. It was a kind of rattle in the Middle East. The Egyptians used this in the ceremonies dedicated to Isis.

Herbert Lockyer described it as a bent rod of iron in a horseshoe shape with cross bars on which rings were placed, causing it to rattle when shaken. Systrums were included in the celebration enacted when the ark was being moved.

> David and all Israel were celebrating with all their might before the Lord, with castanets, harps, lyres, timbrels, systrums and cymbals.
> *(2 Samuel 6:5)*

Percussion instruments were used in temple worship by the Levites.

Percussion Instruments Today

The percussion player is the only musician who makes noises as well as musical sounds. Andre Previn (1983) notes:

> The percussion section is sometimes called the kitchen department. Shakespeare refers to the percussive use of the tongs, bones, and saltbox. Pots and pans were used at the time by the less well-off as makeshift instruments. From

kitchen department the term passed onto kettledrums with their bowls and cymbals reminiscent of pan lids.

Percussion instruments are an integral part of the modern orchestra, rock music, and jazz, as well as traditional folk music.

Conclusion

Tracing all music and instruments back to God and his glorious kingdom humbles us, and helps us to understand all the Lord has made available throughout the history of humankind.

The revelation of God's creation of Lucifer, that perfect musical being, from which has flowed the most indescribable music throughout all the heavens, is mind-blowing.

But Lucifer despised his Creator and sought to use his many accomplishments to eventually lead humankind into the worst type of behaviour. The result of this was that music became one of the many struggles that humankind has had to deal with in its fallen state.

From there, it has been possible for us to understand the fine art of music more fully, from its beginning, to what is available on our earth today.

7. THE FALL OF LUCIFER

Lucifer in his creation was endowed with many gifts, which mere humans would have desired. He was given great intelligence, free will, personality which attracted others to him and was the personification of the highest form of music. His apparel was glorious, displaying his high ranks in heaven. These ranks included guardian of the throne and music director.

Unfortunately, pride entered his heart. From that point Isaiah clearly described the descent of Lucifer from his position in the heaven:

> All your pomp has been brought down to the grave, along with your harps. How you have fallen from heaven, morning star, son of the dawn! You have been cast down to the earth, you who once laid low the nations! You said in your heart, 'I will ascend to the heavens; I will raise my throne above the stars of God; I will ascend above the tops of the clouds; I will make myself like the Most High.' But you are brought down to the realm of the dead, to the depth of the pit.
> *(Isaiah 14:11–15)*

There are other verses in the New Testament which appear to be alluding to Isaiah's verses on the fall of Satan. Jesus tells his disciples: *I beheld Satan as lightning fall from heaven* (Luke 10:18 KJV). John writes: *I saw a star fall from heaven unto the earth: and to him was given the key of the bottomless pit* (Revelation 9:1 KJV).

Unfortunately, pride filled the heart of this great eternal being – a being full of all the wonder, through which the creator God could express his creative powers – powerful, beautiful, and skilled in so many activities. Many a human being would crave to be empowered with just one of these amazing skills. This pride rose in his heart and led him into a state of arrogance and high-mindedness.

Sir Thomas Browne's (1605–1682) words (as cited in McAdoo, 1991):

> For him, charity is the heart of religious practice without which faith is a mere notion, and he counts himself fortunate that he has escaped the temptation to pride (a mortal enemy to Charity), the first and father-sin.

With this, the greatest act of pride, chaos, was not only experienced through the courts of heavens itself but the chaos, when it exploded, soon infiltrated throughout all God's creation of the earth.

All the fine arts have suffered, becoming part of this contamination. Whatever the strata of society, from the highest in the land to the lowest, depravity has penetrated throughout by means of the arts and music.

There is little we can add to describe Lucifer's attempt to glorify himself, and the results of that glorification. He was considered the most superior archangel with the greatest powers.

He had many disciples who followed him even though their end would be so pointless. 2 Samuel 1:27 describes this fall! *Oh, how the mighty have fallen.*

E Royston Pike in his comments on *Paradise Lost* in *100 Great Books* (Milton, 1974) writes:

> Until recently (we are given to understand) Satan had held an honourable post in the courts of heaven, perhaps even as the second-in-command to the Highest.
>
> But when God indicated his preference for his only son, Satan had raised impious war in heaven, with the result that he and all the angels who had supported him and had durst defy the omnipotent to arms were hurl'd headlong flaming from the ethereal sky, with hideous ruin and combustion, to bottomless perdition.

Many of Satan's followers are described by Milton (1974) in *Paradise Lost* as the 'Lords of the World'.

- Prince, O chief of many throned powers who include the many deities set up by humans of every race and tongue.
- Moloch, horrid king besmeared with blood of human sacrifice and parent's tears.
- Astarte, Queen of Heav'n worshipped by the Phoenicians.
- Isis and Osiris – gods of Egypt – were their priest and priestess who controlled the masses by sorceries and evil deeds.
- The many Greek and Roman gods: Zeus and Jupiter

– both king of the gods; Hera and Juno – gods of marriage; Artemis and Diana – gods of hunting; Dionysus and Bacchus – gods of wine.

And so, the list goes on to include the many gods and goddesses have who captured the hearts of humans throughout the ages and continue to do so even in this modern time. The Jews were not the only ones who bowed the knee to Baal.

The result has been that many who followed these idols have become incapable of discerning right from wrong. Instead, they have been drawn down from the loftiness of silence and beauty into ideas of noise, mindlessness and poorness of spirit. This state of mind has continued throughout history and is clear even today.

Satanic Forces Throughout the Ages

Satan's power has continued, even challenging our Saviour Jesus for forty days in the wilderness. Since then, we have witnessed his continuous destruction of humankind from within the humble home to glorious palaces.

Nations have been at war throughout history, bringing about the destruction of millions of people, together with the abuse of innocent children. Justice and peace have been abandoned in favour of rights for everyone regardless of how evil they might be.

Throughout his life, the great reformer, Martin Luther (1483–1546), struggled with despair, during which time he often felt Satan was close by, chasing him. He called this experience *anfechtung* (contest) which R G Sproul (2011) in his book *Unseen Realities*, 'The Adversity' p. 143, named as the unbridled, relentless assault and attack that the prince of darkness brought against him.

Sproul continues, "Had the Devil won these assaults with Luther, then the Reformation may have not taken place."

As Martin Luther was a fine musician, he reintroduced congregational singing in his services. He firmly believed that sacred music has a power that as he says, 'drives out the devil and makes people cheerful'.

Luther's 'A Might Fortress Is Our God' (c.1529), because of its power and resolution, was named the catchcry of the Battle Hymn of the Reformation Movement. This hymn is a paraphrase of Psalm 46:1 and 11: *God is our refuge and strength, an ever-present help in trouble ... The Lord Almighty is with us; The God of Jacob is our fortress*, and the hymn still remains popular with believers today.

In those tumultuous times after Luther's death, Philip Melanchthon encouraged the believers to sing the song 'A Mighty Fortress', reminding them that it gave to each of them the strength to resist the devil.

It is good to note that throughout all this mayhem and destruction, there were many angels who did not bow the knee to Lucifer. Prior to the creation of Adam and Eve these angels remained loyal to their God.

A MIGHTY FORTRESS IS OUR GOD

A mighty fortress is our God, a bulwark never failing;
Our helper He, amid the flood of mortal ills prevailing.
For still our ancient foe doth seek to work us woe;
His craft and pow'r are great, and armed with cruel hate
On earth is not his equal.

And tho' this world, with devils filled,
should threaten to undo us
We will not fear, for God hath willed
His truth to triumph thru us,
The prince of darkness grim – we tremble not for him
His rage we can endure, for, lo! His doom is sure
One little word shall fell Him.

That word above all earthly powers, no thanks to them, abideth
The Spirit and the gifts are ours,
through Him who with us sideth.
Let goods and kindred go, this mortal life also;
The body they may kill, God's truth abideth still
His Kingdom is forever.

Conclusion
Summary of Chapters 1–7

All who love the Lord wait for the second coming of Christ and peace on earth. To understand this coming event more fully, all need be aware of the pre-dawn of creation where the journey of life commenced.

As we continue this journey into the creation of humankind with its special environment, tailor-made for our existence, may we all be enlivened to again seek God and rejoice in His wonderful creation.

8. THE FIRST HEAVEN

Preparation of the Earth and its Surroundings

The book of Genesis is a drama on a large scale. Chapters 1–11 supply a general history of humankind over thousands of years. Although creation is described as taking place in six days, it is thought by some that those days may represent a pattern expressing the creative energy and completeness to God's satisfaction. Each act of God was perfect in its execution and shows the orderliness and uniformity of God's work.

Although many wish to believe that all the wonder and beauty around us happened by chance, it is reassuring to each Christian to recognise that there is an intelligent design and order throughout the universe. The elements necessary for this amazing place came into being step by step until it was perfect for our existence. As far as humans are aware there is no other place where we could live and survive in the whole of the universe. Nehemiah writes:

> You alone are the Lord, you made the heavens, even the
> highest heavens, and all their starry host, the earth and
> all that is on it, the seas and that is in them. You gave life
> to everything, and the multitudes of heaven.
> *(Nehemiah 9:6)*

At the Beginning

Genesis 1 begins with a simple yet majestic statement confirming that God created the heavens and the earth. The terms heaven and earth are ancient Hebrew words which convey the concept of the universe. All came into being through God's word with no pre-existing materials. All things include the sun, moon, and stars – which became objects of heathen worship.

In Genesis 1:1–2, the Hebrew words used for the first stages of the creation of the cosmos are *tohu* 'trackless waste', *bohu* 'a great expanse of emptiness' and *tehom* 'a watery abyss' which Jordan Peterson (2019) describes "as a formless potential from which the God of Genesis called forth order, using the same language at the beginning of time".

From this point, the commencement of creation took place as the Spirit of God hovered over the watery abyss (Glynn, 1996).

Epic cosmology was accepted by Canaan, Syria, and Mesopotamia. In these creation myths of Israel's neighbours, there was always a battle between their so-called good god, like Baal or Marduk, and an evil being which dwelt in the waters of Chaos.

This battle between the forces of good and evil, as covered in Genesis, and other references later in the Bible, resulted in the fall of Satan (the evil one), who was in existence before the creation. The Book of Daniel records a number of conflicts. From thence, the battle has continued throughout the being and experience of humankind.

Stories of national epics and myths have been used over the centuries for retelling past histories and spiritual truths and are still in print today. Like C S Lewis (1898–1963) in *The Chronicles of Narnia* and G K Chesterton (1874–1936) who with his great imagination was a master of this genre. He used ancient mythology together with fact to express realities in an alternative way and to encourage readers to consider the great works of God a little more deeply.

Day 1 – Bringing Light and Darkness into Being

> "Let there be light", and there was light. God saw that the light was good, and he separated light from darkness. God called the light day and the darkness he called night, and there was evening and there was morning – the first day.
> *(Genesis 1:3–5)*

This separation of day from night is the commencement of time as we know it (Millard, 2009). Separating day and night may appear chronologically out of order here, as they are described before the sun, moon, and stars, but (chronology) as a modern idea, would not have been in the mind of the writer. He describes a number of events, which together give us a whole picture of time as we know it.

The main message here is that God continued to perfect each aspect of creation until it was suitable to cover our existence and the maintenance of every living thing great or small.

As with so many spiritual truths which are revealed at this point, light had a dual purpose, not only to introduce time, but reaffirming the belief that light is part of the glory of God.

John Macarthur (2005) penned, "Light is that which most clearly reveals and most closely approximates God's glory".

Like him, Daniel confirms this belief:

> Praise be to the name of God for ever and ever. Wisdom and power are His. He changes times and seasons, He removes kings and sets up kings, He reveals deep and hidden secret things. He knows what lies in darkness, and light dwells with Him.
> *(Daniel 2:20–22)*

Day 2 – Earth's Atmosphere

Genesis 1:6–8 records the separation of the heavens and the earth. This scene describes a vast expanse which contains a protective layer overlaying the earth and divides the waters below from the waters above. Here, between the heavens and the earth, the earth's breathable atmosphere is held.

Josephus (37–38/1987) scripted of the events of the second day, "After this, on the second day, he placed the heaven over the whole world, and separated it from the other parts; and he decided it should stand by itself. He also placed a crystalline (firmament) around it and put it together in a manner agreeable to the earth and fitted it for giving moisture and rain for affording the advantage of dews."

This may not be a great scientific explanation of that

catastrophic event, but it explains the creation of watering the earth, in preparation for plant life.

Day 3 – Creation of Trees and Plant Life

As the waters gathered, fashioning the oceans, lakes, rivers, and streams, the dry land appeared, and the earth became habitable. With the availability of land and water it was possible to grow the necessary commodities. Vegetation, like grain and fruit sprung up, making the earth suitable for the continuation of life on earth.

But the creation of vegetation did not end there. Exotic trees and flowers covered the ground, transforming the new world into a kaleidoscope of shapes and colours which remain even today. Each plant, regardless of type, was fully grown, with its own seed within itself for propagation of the species (Genesis 1:9–13).

Day 4 – Creation of Time – Sun, Moon and Stars

Prior to God creating time, the whole of the universe was a place without limits. This is called 'infinity', limitless time, space, or distance, a place where it was impossible for humans to survive.

On the fourth day God continued to develop more light sources to brighten the day and night; the sun lightens each day, and the moon and stars are revealed each night. God then showed further purposes for which they were created: separating the days from the night, becoming signs to mark days and years, creating the seasons, and marking the sacred times.

Josephus (37–38/1987) commented on this: "On the fourth day he adorned the heaven with the sun, the moon, and the other stars, and appointed them their motions and courses that the vicissitudes of the seasons might be clearly signified."

The placement of the stars created a heavenly panorama, which has never ceased to delight people throughout the ages. No human lighting display has ever come close to the glitter and sparkle of God's handiwork which inspires and comforts all humanity throughout the darkness of night. As well as being wonderful to behold, the moon and stars have been a practical addition to the sky, navigating many a mariner to a haven when the sea appeared endless.

Travellers through the world have been guided by knowledge of the rising of the sun – depicting east to west – which led to the invention of the compass.

As with so many other creative activities, the lights were not only to be used as signs to aid us, but God used this cycle of time as an expression of eternal faithfulness. From times of early civilizations to our present time, this cycle has not been broken. This is what the Lord says:

> If I have not made my covenant with day and night and established the laws of heaven and earth, then I will reject the descendants of Jacob and David.
> *(Jeremiah 33:25–26)*

This promise not only concerns Israel but is also relevant to the whole world.

Lord of Time

Mitch and Zhava Glaser (1987) commenced their book, *The Fall Feasts of Israel*, by considering the reason for the creation of time:

> In the beginning, God created time. He made the light and darkness, calling the light day and the darkness night: And there was evening and there was morning, one day. Yet the Holy One is eternal and lives beyond the limitations of time and space. He created time – a sequence of events to serve as the arena where the heavenly meets the temporal, where God meets man. By his act of creation, the sovereign of eternity, was also crowned the Lord of time.

The creation of time made our planet suitable for all our needs prior to and after the fall. The sun is not needed in heaven because of the light which emanates out of His holy presence. He and His earlier creations do not require rest; their bodies are immortal. Their tasks did not leave them emotionally and physically replete!

On the other hand, all earthly living creatures require a time cycle: day and night, work and rest. These verses remind us of our worth here on earth, as well as telling again that our destiny is assured when we are translated to heaven for eternity.

Day 5 – Introduction of Marine Life and Fowl

These events appear so minor considering the countless birds and marine animals which cover the earth. From the tiny sparrows to the grandeur of flamingos, and from the minnows of the sea to the great sperm whales who share our ocean, our awareness of these creatures helps us respect and understand in a more meaningful way our Creator God (Genesis 1:2023).

Day 6 – Creation of Land Animals and Humans

During this final day, all living creatures that can be catalogued into their specific species appeared – sea creatures and birds, and land-based animals, which are then divided into wild animals and domestic animals. Another group which made its appearance at this time included those who crawled along the ground – snakes, lizards, mammals, and insects (Genesis 1:20–25).

Then came humans who became the pinnacle of God's creation:

> And God created mankind in our own image, in our likeness, so that they may rule over the fish of the sea and the birds in the sky, over the livestock and all wild animals, and all the creatures that move along the ground.
> *(Genesis 1:26)*

Day 7 – Creation is Complete

God rested on the seventh day and blest it. This is the only time in the Bible that God rested. The creation story would have percolated into other nations and cultures if we believe all life came from God.

There is evidence of a seventh day of rest in an Egyptian

creation account from Memphis, which says the god Ptah rested after the completion of his work. Similar stories are found in Mesopotamia where the gods rested after the creation of humans. God resting on the seventh day confirmed the pattern for the work cycle of humans. Later, Moses based the law of Sabbath Rest as the finale of the creation week.

The Goodness of God's Creation

God himself is good – the Father, Son and the Holy Spirit are good!

Before we move on to Adam and Eve, we are able to pause here to observe that the creation story was developed around six declarations that God saw it was good (Genesis 1:4, 10, 12, 21, 25). On the sixth day God saw everything he had made, and it was very good.

Cecil Frances Alexander a mid-eighteenth century composer, was a born teacher who wrote many hymns as teaching aids to educate children in the Christian faith. In this role, she worked beside her husband in the daily running of his church. Other Christian workers throughout the world still attest to the suitability of her songs as a means of teaching.

The composition of the hymn 'All Things Bright and Beautiful' came about when her godsons complained to her that learning the catechism was boring. Alexander decided to help them and she set about writing a series of poems on the catechism to aid the children to remember each part of the Nicene Creed.

The first belief of the catechism is "I believe in God the

Father, who hath made me, and all the world". The song begins and ends with the refrain, 'All Things Bright and Beautiful' which thus reiterates treasured heavenly truths (Houghton, 1982).

After seeing some of the beautiful scenes all around, Alexander then affirmed that God is the creator of all these things. Throughout the world, generations of Jews and Christians have used repetition in verses and choruses of songs to teach their children about God and His salvation.

Although written for the children of her parish church, thousands of children since that time have continued to acclaim this heavenly truth.

Recently a Chinese-Malay friend, who as a child lived in a cathedral where her grandfather was the Dean, confided in me that she loved hearing her son, a pianist, play 'All Things Bright and Beautiful', which had been a favourite hymn during her childhood in Malaya.

The music, which is still popular today, was written by the songwriter W H Monk who was a skilled musician. He was also the first editor of *Hymns Ancient and Modern*, one of the first hymn books published in 1861. The hymn commences by announcing some of the inexpressible wonders and perfection of creation.

ALL THINGS BRIGHT AND BEAUTIFUL

All things bright and beautiful,
All creatures great and small,
All things wise and wonderful –
The Lord God made them all.

Each little flower that opens,
Each little bird that sings –
He made their glowing colours,
He made their tiny wings.

The purple headed mountain,
The river running by,
The sunset and the morning
That brightens up the sky.

The cold wind in the winter,
The pleasant summer sun,
The ripe fruits in the garden –
He made them everyone.

He gave us eyes to see them,
And lips that we might tell
How great is God Almighty,
Who has made all things well.

All things bright and beautiful,
All creatures great and small.
All things wise and wonderful –
The Lord God made them all.

Conclusion

From the creation of the whole earth, we now move on to the central players in this creation drama; Adam and Eve, who were placed in a beautiful garden with instructions to take care of this wonderful place.

It was also the place where God Himself could fellowship with them.

9. CREATION OF HUMANKIND

In the Image of God, He Created Them

During the six days of creation, we see the Lord as director of the drama of creation, drawing together elements for staging of the universe and the earth. During day six he completed the final scenario of this great work with the introduction of the pinnacle of creation – humankind.

The first three days supply a backdrop for the drama, and during the last three days the actors in the Creation drama are introduced:

Day 1: Light, separated from darkness creating day and night

Day 2: The separation of the heavenly atmosphere and water below

Day 3: Land and seas separated, making way for vegetation

Day 4: Sun, moon and stars

Day 5: Birds and fish

Day 6: Land creatures and humankind, who became the climax of the entire creative week

Day 7: Creation is completed and God rests (Wilmington, 1985).

A quote from an unknown source which expresses God's delight in Adam and Eve, the pinnacle of His creation, says "Our God speaks as the Creator-king, by announcing his crowning work to the members of his heavenly court".

The six days of creation describe the formation of both living and non-living things, placed in a massive interdependent ecosystem that sustains and supports life. However, the crowning glory of this arrangement was the introduction of Adam, a human.

While the creation of the first six days reflected God's creative abilities, Adam was described as being made in God's image (in Latin, *imago dei*). This theological term, which applied uniquely to humans, expresses the symbolical relation between God and humanity. It recognises special qualities of human in human nature which enables God to be manifest in humans.

If humans recognise this unity with God, then they are in a position for God to work His purposes and plans through their lives. Humans with this understanding are able learn to love God, and through Him they are capable of loving others. This likeness to God was so entrenched that even the downfall could not eradicate it.

> His divine power has given us everything we need for a godly life. We are made partakers of the divine nature, receiving, and sharing God's own nature through his promises. Then we must work that divine nature into our human nature by developing godly habits.
> *(1 Peter 1–2)*

Unfortunately, many people throughout the world have used the gifts they have been given to cause chaos and destruction to themselves and other humans, as well as being determined throughout the ages to seek to destroy the earth itself.

Now to the man Adam himself; what was Adam really like? Though he was the highlight of God's creation, he had a limited ability in this life to understand many things. For instance, we humans are unable to see the total colour spectrum displayed by certain elements of nature – we cannot naturally see ultraviolet and infrared light sources – but we do know now that some animals, fish and birds can.

Humans are also unable to hear certain high and low range sound patterns that many other animals are able to hear easily. For example, dogs and bats can hear ultra-high frequency sounds denied to us without sophisticated and sensitive equipment.

Josephus (37–38/1987) wrote:

> Moses, after the seventh day was over, begins to talk philosophically; and concerning the formation of man, says thus: That God took the dust from the ground and formed man, and instilled in him a spirit and a soul.

Josephus then continued:

> God also presented the living creatures, when he had made them, according to their kinds, both male and female, to Adam.

Creation of Marriage

After the creation of Adam, God was aware of Adam's need for a companion who could share his life, his faith and his responsibilities. *But for Adam, no suitable helper was found* (Genesis 2:20). God's final creative act was Eve, who was created out of the body of Adam. *Adam said, "This is now bone of my bones, and flesh of my flesh; she shall be called Woman, because she was taken out of Man"* (Genesis 2:23 KJV).

God delighted in his love for his final creation, by implanting in each the likeness of God, *So God created mankind in His own image, in the image of God He created them; male and female He created them* (Genesis 1:27).

Throughout human history, communities have always had some type of marriage ceremony which was a contract between a man and woman. No matter how primitive or wealthy the people were, the married couple was responsible for the protection and care of their children and the elderly. They also were accountable to join with other members of their community, protecting them from marauders and other groups who would seek to annihilate them.

It is interesting to watch animals and see how they also work together to care for their families. When a baby elephant is born the other females are around to help keep the baby safe. Many other groups have a dominant male or female who is in charge of the group.

To those who worship the creator God, marriage is a holy sacrament, as it was the first commandment from the Lord uniting the man with a woman, thus creating an eternal bond.

The result of this union is followed by this: *That is why a man leaves his father and mother and is united to his wife, and they become one flesh* (Genesis 2:24).

Throughout the Scriptures, the Lord confirms marriage as His perfect gift. One such verse which embraces this is in Malachi, when the people queried why they were being judged by God. Malachi replies:

> You ask why? It is because the Lord is acting as a witness between you and the wife of your youth because you have broken faith with her, though she is your partner and the wife of your marriage covenant. Has not the Lord made them one? In flesh and spirit, they are his. And why one? Because he was seeking godly offspring.
> *(Malachi 2:13–16)*

The Sacrament of Marriage has come down in history as one of the five additional sacraments following baptism and holy communion in the Anglican Church. In the sacrament of marriage, through the joining of hands and the giving and receiving of vows and rings, a man and woman become a sign of a much deeper inward reality, their life together becomes a sacrament of love (Brady, 1983).

Procreation

Although Adam and Eve equally shared God's image, they, by divine design, were physically different to enable them to propagate. Neither one could carry this out without the other:

God blessed then, and God said unto them, "Be fruitful and multiply, and replenish the earth" (Genesis 1:28 KJ21).

The Divine Revealed in the Human

In his book *Exploring Scripture*, Rev Philip J Cunningham (1992) asks two questions:

1. Can we ignore the human context of sacred scripture? Would this not be to neglect something equally fundamental? We read: *God created mankind in his image, in the image of God He created them; male and female He created them* (Genesis 1:27).
2. Is there not a sense in which the divine is revealed in the human, not in any crudely anthropocentric manner, such as through an idol, or as a god in human form, but through the humans, without distorting the human?

William Shakespeare, in his work *Hamlet* (as cited in Belsey, 2012), includes the phrase, "What a piece of work is man, how noble in reason, how infinite in faculties? In form and moving how expressive and admirable, in action like an Angel. In apprehension how like a god. The beauty of the world, the paragon of animals." This describes the beauty and wonder of God's favoured creation, and yet, Hamlet understands our life on earth is transitional. It will not become immortal until we reach our heavenly abode.

Shakespeare continues: 'And yet to me, what is this quintessence of dust?' Here Hamlet reminds one and all that we are mortal, and our mortal bodies will return to the earth in this life. But life goes on as we continue to repopulate!

The awareness of our importance to God humbles me when it comes to the interaction I have with those around me. No matter whether a person is great or small, they are to be honoured simply because of their heritage.

This does not extend to those who have given themselves over to Satan, and work with him to destroy not only people, but all of God's creation.

Conclusion

The creation of humankind brought the whole of God's creation together. Firstly, as special creatures, which having the image of God implanted in each, meant that all have the capacity to love and worship the creator. Then secondly, as caretakers of the wonderful world in which all are privileged to exist.

> Welcome all wonders in one sight,
> Eternity in a span,
> Summer in winter, day in night,
> Heaven in earth, and God in man!
> Lifts earth to heaven.

10. THE CREATION

The Oratorio by Joseph Haydn

A wonderful way to round off the creation story is to listen and absorb Haydn's great oratorio *The Creation*. This work is a meditation on the seven days of creation as they unfold in the Biblical account in Genesis. By hearing this great work, which combines the best of human dialogue with heavenly, expressive music, each one can tap into human emotions and experiences, together with a heightened awareness of the glory and wonder of our great creator. Terry Glaspey (2015) documented that, "When his work was composed, in his chapter on the creation, Franz Joseph Haydn (1732–1809) commented, 'It was written to inspire the worship and adoration of the creator'" (as cited in Kavanaugh, 1996).

The oratorio is vivid and powerful in its depiction of the unfolding of the creation story, using Haydn's musical textures to paint the progression of God's creative acts.

Joseph Haydn composed the music, and the libretto came from a number of sources. Although these contributors never met, their thoughts and ideas on the creation were so aligned with one another, that when they were brought together the result was a glorious act of devotion praising God, which we all can share.

It is encouraging for every Christian today to be ever aware of the saints who lived and wrote about our great faith in literature, music and other artistic endeavours, over the centuries. By doing so, they have enabled us to draw nearer to our God.

Today, many of us are so involved with each other and our present surroundings, through social media platforms, that few of us feel the need to expand our vision by taking time to look back and embrace the great men and women of faith from Biblical times to the present. These giants have bequeathed to us many treasures which have become our inheritance, and if embraced, can continue to help place our faith in perspective.

The Librettist – the person who wrote the lyrics

The actual writer of the libretto of *The Creation* is unknown, and possibly will remain so, as the original copy has been lost. Since the original libretto was written in English, it is thought the writer may have been an Englishman called Lidley; others believe it to be Thomas Linley, a promoter of oratorios in London during the eighteenth century. This is a possibility because Linley was experienced in theatrical performances. His sources included excerpts from Milton's Genesis epic *Paradise Lost*, the Psalms, and books from the Apocrypha.

John Milton (1608–1674)

Milton (1674) introduced his work *Paradise Lost* by formally declaring his poem's subject: "Of man's first disobedience, and fruit of that forbidden tree, whose mortal taste brought death into the world, and all our woe, with lost Eden."

He briefly described the acts of creation in Genesis, alluding to these events as being brought into being by the Holy Spirit.

Milton then focused on Adam and Eve's first act of disobedience which introduced the knowledge of good and evil. By the time he wrote this work, Milton was blind and had to dictate it.

He has been described as a person whose characteristics reflected his strong personal convictions and a sense of self-determination. He was deeply passionate about freedom of speech, and freedom of press, for at the time such ideas could have led to loss of life.

The individualism that he displayed was not welcome because the political climate of his day was so volatile. The situation developed into a war between King Charles I and Oliver Cromwell, representing a clash between the king's divine rule and parliament. Some considered the conflict between the king and parliament also pointed to a message of the conflict between heaven and earth.

As a writer and poet, Milton is considered on equal terms with William Shakespeare. John Milton's strongest means of expression was his epic poem in 'blank verse'. Blank verse is a form of poetry dating back to ancient Jewish works as well as that of other ancient nations. This form of unrhymed blank verse developed into classical Roman and Greek literature.

Three Types of Verse

Blank verse is poetry with a strict metre but without a rhyme scheme. Formal verse is poetry with a strict metre (rhythmic pattern) and rhyme scheme. Free verse is poetry without any strict metre or rhyme scheme.

English romantic poets valued this exploration of blank verse as a form which released them from the then popular metrical verse. This included not only freeing it up, but also giving other poets and composers the opportunity to be more inventive in their ideas and expression. Although many poets tried to emulate this method in epic form, only William Wordsworth succeeded when he wrote *The Prelude*.

Many have compared this work to the Roman poet Virgil's *Aeneid*. Although Virgil's epic tale was considered his finest work, it is based on myths and legends, rather than facts. Its storyline, written in twelve volumes, relates to the so-called journey of Aeneas fleeing from the Sack of Troy to Italy where he is said to have founded the city of Rome. In direct contrast to this, Milton's epic was based on one of the greatest events of humanity, that of the creation of the universe and the earth. This work has been recognised as the greatest and grandest epic poem in the English language.

Together with blank verse, Milton used other forms of unconventional rhythm. He used metric verse in his paraphrase of the hymn 'Let us with a gladsome mind' which was composed when he was fifteen years old. It is versification of Psalm 136, a style which dominated the written hymns at the time. The first printing contained twenty-four couplets with a two-line refrain, but over the years most hymn books, in respect of congregations, reduced this number to make it easier to sing. Milton stuck closely to the Scriptures, but generally used language which was graphic and dramatic. These were again altered over time went so as to be more in accordance with the language of later singers. With his passionate personality, hymn-composition was not his forte .

LET US WITH A GLADSOME MIND

Let us, with a gladsome mind
Praise the LORD for he is kind;
For his mercies shall endure,
Ever faithful, ever sure.

He with all-commanding might,
Filled the new made earth with light;
For his mercies shall endure
Ever faithful, ever sure.

The floods stood still like walls of glass,
While the Hebrew bands did pass;
For his mercies shall endure,
Ever faithful, ever sure.

All things living, he doth feed,
His full hand supplies their need;
For his mercies shall endure,
Ever faithful, ever sure.

Franz Joseph Haydn (1732–1809)

Finally, the person whose contribution made this great work a reality was the composer Franz Joseph Haydn. As he was one of the greatest composers in Europe in the years between 1760 and 1820, he had all the attributes needed to drive the vision forward. Not only Christians respect this work; thousands of others throughout the centuries have embraced it as a masterpiece, and it continues to be a favourite even today.

Haydn was raised in a Christian home and later in life expressed his gratitude to his parents for 'bringing him up in the fear of God'. They wished for him to become a priest, but he was sure of his calling and wrote, "I know that God has favoured me, and I recognise it thankfully. I also believe that I have done my duty and have been of use to the world through my works. Let others do the same."

There was a time when he was criticised by some of the more puritanical church members for his overly joyous music. His reply was, 'Since God has given me a cheerful heart, He will forgive me for serving Him cheerfully.'

As he grew, his love for God never wavered, and throughout his life his work and faith were strongly linked. As a result of this, he sought to compose a work which would embody his faith and express his musical ability. The vision he had nurtured for many years became a reality when he heard Handel's *Messiah*. Although he had written much fine church music, after he had experienced this great work he was determined to create something as magnificent, something that not only expressed his musical gifts, but also his faith in God.

Soon the opportunity arose. While Haydn was in London in 1795, the great impresario Salomon suggested that Haydn should set a work called *The Creation* to music. Salomon had intended it for Handel. He showed it to Haydn, who was delighted with the libretto, as he knew this work had specific sentiments and style which could come alive through his music.

This certainly was the case! Haydn caught the spirit of the creation by expressing in the music the scenes which constantly were glimpsed throughout, namely, light and darkness followed by the activities of the many birds, fish, and animals, coming alive through delightful musical motifs.

Haydn composed the score in two years from 1796 to 1798, while in his mid-sixties, which was thought to have been the height of his creative power. Although originally written in English, *The Creation* was later translated into German, and is still sung in both English and German today.

Haydn took the work home to Vienna, and gave it to Baron Gottfried van Swieten, a wealthy amateur musician. In 1800, van Swieten shortened the libretto and translated it into German, making it possible for Haydn to publish the score in German, and then revert it back to the English text.

Haydn was a child of his time! His work was written in strict classical style, and although he was never an innovator it was through his work, developing and enlarging the symphonic form, together with that of classical symphonic orchestration, that he was given the title 'Father of the Symphony'.

Haydn specifically related to God and his church in much of his music. He created a large amount of sacred music including Catholic and English church service music. One hymn tune which has become a firm favourite to many Christians is his *Emperor's Hymn*, known to us today under the name 'Austria'.

For *The Creation* he used the musical style of oratorio, which is an extended setting of a religious libretto written in dramatic form, for choir and orchestra, without scenery, dress, or action, and performed in either a church or concert hall.

Like the old mystery and morality plays, these works made it possible for more people to experience Biblical history, like *The Creation*, as other musical events were only performed in local churches. Many other composers, at this time and later, wrote oratorios to the same pattern.

Joseph Haydn was a composer who saw music in everything. He was at home with inanimate things which he often included in his compositions. One example is *The Clock Symphony*, which is based on the ticking of the clock.

He was forever joyous, regardless of his circumstances, when describing the wonders of *The Creation*, and his joy permeates the work.

Parts of the Oratorio

Overture

The Creation, like operas of those days, begins with an overture. This is an orchestral introduction used to set the stage and action of the drama.

Recitative

This style of vocal composition disregards fixed rhythms, so as to carry the action forward, replicating natural sung speech. The three archangels, Raphael, Uriel, and Gabriel are used to achieve this.

Aria – air
A lengthy and developed vocal piece, generally in three sections, that gives the singer an opportunity to soliloquise what has been declaimed in the recitative.

Chorus
A group of male and female singers in four parts, who generally join the soloists at the end of each section.

The choral sections highlight Haydn at his best. At the end of each day's activities, they raise their voices in praise to God. This music, so beautifully sung, is possibly reminiscent of the joyous sounds in heavenly places. The harmonies are delightful, using many fugal entries that causes the music to weave in and out of the four parts.

Haydn set this oratorio in three parts. The first two parts describe the first six days of creation, the final part takes place on the seventh day when God rested.

Orchestra
Throughout the work, Haydn uses every orchestral device, both musical and structural, of the classical period.

Part the First – Overture

Representation of Chaos
The orchestra begins the overture by expressing a musical painting of Genesis 1:1, *In the beginning God created the heavens and the earth ... and darkness was upon the face of the deep.*

This scene stands for the primeval chaos of the earth. The music moves slowly and softly, then is followed by much flurry, chaotic chords, and agitated movements. These movements, alternating from soft to loud crashing sounds, continue until its completion and all is calm. The work continues to fade away until the last three chords of C minor are sounded in pianissimo. Thus, drama has begun!

Recitative – Bass

Raphael, one of the archangels, announces the story of creation by confirming the progenitor of all this activity to be the Eternal God himself: *In the beginning God created the heavens and the earth; and the earth was without form, and void, and darkness was upon the face of the deep.*

The chorus softly continues the narrative in recitative style, accompanied by the strings of the orchestra playing a soft pizzicato which celebrates the creation of light: *The Spirit of God moved upon the face of the waters, and God said, "Let there be light," and there was light.*

Suddenly the mood changes on the final word 'light', sung with a fortissimo and accompanied by the orchestra which comes crashing onto the scene with the C major chord, then continues in fortissimo. The premier audience was so stunned and surprised by this intense use of contrasting dynamics that the orchestra could not go ahead until the enthusiasm had died down.

Recitative – Tenor

Uriel – "God saw the light, that it was good, and God divided the light from the darkness."

Air

"Now vanish before the holy beams", and Uriel rejoices as the first day appears. "Now chaos ends and order prevails."

Chorus

The chorus continues this glorious theme, accompanied by a soft pizzicato on the strings, celebrating the newly created world.

One the third day, Gabriel announced that God said, *"Let the earth bring forth grass, herb yielding seed, and the fruit tree yielding fruit after its kind, whose seed is in itself, upon the earth,"* and it was so.

Haydn enhanced this act of creation with a lovely pastoral tune, written in compound time, giving a feeling of restfulness and peace to rural scenes. Another great composer who used this idea was Beethoven. He named his sixth symphony *The Pastoral Symphony*:

>With verdure clad and the fields appear,
>Delightful to the ravish'd sense;
>By flowers sweet and gay
>Enhanced is the charming sight.
>Here fragrant herbs their odours shed;
>Here shoots the healing plant;
>With copious fruit the expanded boughs are hung;

In leafy arches twine the shady groves;
O'er lofty hills majestic forests wave.

Commencement of Time

Moving on, the commencement of time is announced by Uriel.

Recitative — Tenor

God said, *"Let there be lights in the firmament of heaven, to divide the day from the night, and to give light upon the earth, and let them be for signs, and for seasons, and for days, and for years."* He made the stars also.

Air: Uriel

Uriel goes on to describe this with wonderful event.

Chorus

"In splendour bright is rising now the sun ." The orchestra portrays a brilliant sunrise, followed by a lesser moonrise. The tune of the sunrise is denoted by ten notes of the D major scale variously harmonised. The moon then rises in the subdominant key of G major, also with a rising passage. Thus, the world is now ready for the main event – the creation of humankind.

Part the First — Finale

The finale of Part the First is the wonderful anthem sung by the choir glorifying God and his majestic work. The text used here is based on Psalm 19:1–3:

The heavens declare the glory of God;
the skies proclaim the work of his hands.
Day after day they pour forth speech;
night after night they reveal knowledge.
They have no speech; they use no words;
No sound is heard from them.

This Psalm 19:1–3 had been used by Bach as the opening chorus of his Cantata BWV 76:
The heavens are telling the glory of God,
The wonder of His work displays the firmament.
To-day that is coming speaks it the day,
The night that is gone to following night
In all the lands resounds the word,
Never unperceived, ever understood.

Part the Second

Part the Second begins with a recitative that continues the storyline.

Recitative: Gabriel

Gabriel begins with a declaration of the creative activity of God: "God said, 'Let the waters bring forth abundantly moving creatures that hath life, and fowl that may fly above the earth in the open firmament of heaven'."

Air: Gabriel

Gabriel continues the story with the aria 'On Mighty Pens'. Here, Haydn comes into his own, musically describing the idiosyncrasies of each of the four birds: the eagle, the lark, the dove, and the nightingale. The eagle soars high on the drafts of wind which the music imitates by soaring up to the upper F. It then continues to the A above, as the eagle's swift flight takes it upwards towards the blazing sun.

The music changes as the eagle welcomes the lark. The dove then joins the merriment by calling his mate, cooing lightly, represented by trills, triplets, and other motifs, that add further colour to the overall picture.

Later, the nightingale, 'the songbird', sings a delightful aria that is echoed by a beautiful soprano song:

> On mighty pens uplifted soars the eagle aloft,
> and cleaves the sky in swiftest flight to the blazing sun.
> The merry lark bids welcome to the morn,
> And cooing, calls the tender dove his mate.
> From every bush and grove
> resound the nightingale's delightful, liquid notes.
> No grief affected yet her breast,
> nor to a mournful tale were tun'd
> her soft enchanting lays.

Recitative: Raphael

"God said, 'Let the earth bring forth the living creatures after its kind, cattle, and creeping thing, and beast of the earth after his kind'."

Raphael sings a lively air describing this scene with the animals – a tawny lion, the nimble stag, then finally, "in long dimension creeps, with sinuous trace, the worm". These are all delightfully depicted using musical motifs and ideas.

Air: Raphael

This thriving part of creation comes to a fitting end with the Air:

> Now heaven in fullest glory shone;
> Earth smil'd in all her rich attire;
> The room of air with fowl is fill'd;
> The water swell'd by shoals of fish;
> By heavy beasts, the ground is trod;
> But all the work was not complete;
> There wanted yet that wond'rous being,
> That, grateful, should God's pow'r admire,
> With heart and voice his goodness praise.

Adam and Eve

The two final characters sing beautiful love songs to each other and praise God for all he has given them.

Recitative: Uriel – God Created Man

> God created man in His own image,
> In the image of God created He him:
> Male and female created He them.
> He breathed into his nostrils the breath of life,
> And man became a living soul.

Air: Uriel

Uriel expands on the recitative with the air, in native worth. Thus, describing this created being in his full glory straight from the heart of God:

> In native worth and honour clad,
> With beauty, courage, strength, adorn'd,
> Erect, with front serene, he stands
> A man, the Lord and king of nature all.

The lyrics continue in rhetoric praising this majestic being:

> His large and arched brow sublime,
> Wisdom deep declared the seat!
> And in his eyes with brightness shines
> The soul, the breath and image of his God.

The created woman is now introduced leaning on his breast:

> With fondness leans upon his breast
> The partner for him form'd,
> A woman, fair and graceful spouse.
> Her softly smiling virgin looks,
> Of flowery spring the mirror
> Bespeak him love, and joy, and bliss.

Part the Third – God's Response

Recitative: Uriel

Uriel concludes the creative event by describing God's response to His creation (Genesis 1:31):

And God saw ev'ry thing that he had made, and behold,
it was particularly good: and the heavenly choir, in song
divine, thus closed the sixth day.

Chorus

Achieved is the glorious work;
The Lord beholds it, and is pleas'd.
In lofty strains let us rejoice,
Our song let be the praise of God.

Conclusion

I highly recommend every reader of this book watch *The Creation* in concert. It aptly demonstrates how creation continues to ever be in the hearts of Jews and Christians alike. I suggest that the listener procures a copy of the libretto and the music, thus making it possible to become involved not only through dialogue, but also through the drama of music that Haydn so brilliantly expressed.

> By thee with bliss, O bounteous Lord,
> both heav'n and earth are stored.

11. THE FALL
Paradise Lost

The most delightful experience given to Adam and Eve was the privilege of walking with God in the cool of the evening. These times of fellowship could have been an opportunity for them to understand, to a limited degree, the nature and person of God and the love he had bestowed on them, as well as the gift of the Garden of Eden. God trusted them, but unfortunately they did not reciprocate.

One of the gifts endowed to Adam and Eve was self-determination, which enabled them to make their own choices. In this perfect environment designed for their own good, there was one tree in the middle of the garden whose fruit God had forbidden them to eat. This prohibition may not appear to be consistent with God's goodness, but God had given these two antagonists so much, and this prohibition involved nothing that would in any way mar their life or happiness.

The Tempter

> Now the serpent was more crafty than any of the wild animals the LORD God had made. He said to the woman, "Did God really say, 'You must not eat from any tree in the garden'?" The woman said to the serpent, "We may eat fruit from the trees in the garden, but God

did say, 'You must not eat fruit from the tree that is in the middle of the garden, and you must not touch it, or you will die.' "You will not certainly die," the serpent said to the woman.
(Genesis 3:1–4)

Through this cunning means, Satan, depicted as the serpent, manipulated Eve to disobey the commandment of God by doing what had been forbidden.

There was nothing harmful in the tree itself; this was a real tree with special properties to impart the knowledge of good and evil. Through the serpent Satan, Eve began by doubting God's word. Then, to make matters worse, Eve added to God's word. Eve yielded to the words of Satan, and Adam yielded to the words of Eve! With this added knowledge of good and evil, Adam and Eve were ashamed of their nakedness and hid from God. As with all the others, including Satan, Adam and Eve could not escape the judgement of God.

Up until this point, apart from the fall of Satan, we have only seen those attributes of God which were directly involved in His creative acts. These attributes include His power and wisdom together with a love of goodness, beauty, and peace.

Because of God's holiness, sin can never be allowed to come into His presence, so must be dealt with accordingly. Adam and Eve jointly disobeyed God with catastrophic results. Not only did they fall from grace, but this sin and suffering led to death and this affected them and all humankind.

As written in Job 14:1 *Mortals, born of woman, are of few*

days and full of trouble. Before the finality of death, this trouble included suffering during childbirth, all kinds of diseases, disorderly conduct in the home, and strife between the nations on earth. The curse also fell upon God's creation. To Adam he said:

> Because you listened to your wife and ate fruit from the tree about which I commanded you, "You must not eat from it," cursed is the ground because of you; through painful toil you will eat food from it all the days of your life.
> *(Genesis 3:17)*

Suddenly thorns, thistles and other weeds appeared, making Adam and Eve's home a wilderness and an unsuitable place in which to live. The Apostle Paul writes: *We know that the whole creation has been groaning as in the pains of childbirth right up to the present time* (Romans 8:22). The situation worsened when they were driven from the Garden, be it for their own protection, for they could not continue eternally in such a state.

Creation's Darkest Hour

During the Second World War, when things were going badly for the Allies, Winston Churchill named this period 'our darkest hour'. The darkest hour also describes an earlier time in history when Adam and Eve doubted God and disobeyed him.

From living in the beautiful Garden of Eden to suddenly being thrust out into a world of chaos was a traumatic experience for Adam and Eve. From that moment on they needed all their strength and ingenuity to survive. This event not only became a tragedy with dire consequences for both of them, but it also severely affected all living things who continued to inhabit the earth.

An image of the eternal goes beyond the reproduction of plants and animals breeding their own kind. Human beings, who share similar physical characteristics and the basic nature of their parents, also inherit the image of God. Therefore, we are confronted with a dichotomy of the inheritance of being human with the image of God. This additional gift not only prepares each person to have the ability to be God's representative on earth, but also to be able to act like Him. The tools humanity has been given for this task include love and caring, conscience, self-awareness and spiritual discernment.

A well-known English hymnwriter and retired priest, Timothy Dudley-Smith, born in 1926, wrote a hymn which reminds us of 'the fall' and its results in a true and sensitive manner.

Commencing in verse one, Dudley-Smith describes the dichotomy of our human existence – made in the image of God, but with the fallen nature bequeathed by Adam and Eve. The hymn describes the results of 'the fall' to us, but there is a promise that God will, in his time, redeem us by his eternal love and sacrifice.

This act of disobedience was not the end! Genesis is known as the book of beginnings, and that includes the continuation of the life of human beings. After Adam and Eve were banished from the Garden of Eden, cherubim with flaming swords stood guard to ensure these fallen humans did not eat fruit from the Tree of Life. This meant that their whole existence depended upon their ability to cope, and this they did.

Humans continued to sustain the earth, but in a different manner. Their lifestyle was one of extreme toil and heartbreak. They endured pain and suffering because suddenly they were on their own and no longer wholly dependent upon their God for survival. It is remarkable how quickly they adapted to their new environment.

The world continued to be an amazing place!

All around there is evidence of God's glorious creation extending from the heavens and embracing our wonderful earth. Since the fall, humans have kept their state as being created in the image of God, thus maintaining the innate ability to reflect, reassess a situation, and plan for whatever is necessary for their survival.

This likeness, together with their DNA, continue in all the children of Adam and Eve as is recorded in the story of Seth:

> When Adam had lived 130 years, he had a son in own likeness, in his own image; and he named him Seth.
> *(Genesis 5:3)*

THE LORD MADE MAN; THE SCRIPTURES TELL

The Lord made man, the Scriptures tell,
To bear his image and his sign;
Yet we by nature share as well
The ancient mark of Adam's line.

In Adam's fall falls every man,
With every gift the father gave;
The crown of all creation's plan,
Became a rebel and a slave.

Herein all woes are brought to birth,
All aching hearts, and sunless skies
Brightness is gone from all the earth,
The innocence of nature dies.

Yet Adam's children, born to pain
By self-enslaved, by sin enticed
Still may by grace be born again
Children of God, beloved in Christ.

In Christ is Adam's ransom met
Earth, by his cross, is holy ground
Eden indeed is with us yet
In Christians are life and freedom found!

Conclusion

As history continues, the battle between good and evil persists, requiring humans to live with constant struggle .

The first choice is to seek to live close to the eternal God; the second choice is to take the easier road full of the attractions of the great deceiver.

However, as we move on, when things appear the darkest, God raises up courageous men and women who strive to protect both humans and the beauty of the world from being decimated by evil forces.

Throughout the ages, the battle between good and evil has been rampant and continues to be, but it is encouraging to know the Lord is victorious and His righteousness and justice will prevail.

> Righteousness and justice are the foundations of your throne. Love and faithfulness go before you.

12. CAIN AND ABEL

The First Sacrifices

Primitive Worship

The very first act of worship in Genesis reveals that from the beginning there was a proper and improper way to worship. This was confirmed when brothers Cain and Abel both used the prescribed method of sacrifice, but only one was accepted. Being so close to God through their mother and father, it can be expected that both sons were aware that sacrificing the firstborn animal was pleasing to God.

This notion is acknowledged by John Macarthur (2005) who wrote in his Bible commentary that both sons may have been given prior knowledge from God as to his acceptable sacrifice. Furthermore, Dr William D Maxwell (1945) began his book *An Outline of Christian Worship* by stating that:

> Worship consists of our words and actions, the outward expression in the presence of God. These words and actions are governed by two things: our knowledge of the god or gods whom we worship, and the human resources we are able to bring to that worship.

This description is true! It supports the notion that little time had passed before humans turned away from the divine object of worship and so altered their sacrifices to suit themselves. It also reinforces the notion that after the fall, death was the only means of pleasing God, with thousands of animals sacrificed becoming a constant reminder of the price for the redemption of humankind.

Cultural Beginnings

Genesis 4:17–22 is an annotated genealogy of humankind, depicting the stirrings in the heart of humanity and the desire to create and develop thoughts, ideas, and activities necessary for survival and enjoyment of their new life.

> Cain made love to his wife, and she ... gave birth to Enoch ... To Enoch was born Irad ... Lamech married two women, Adah gave birth to Jabal ... his brother's name was Jubal... Zillah had a son, Tubal-Cain.
> *(Genesis 4:17–22)*

The world of our earliest ancestors was one of toil and hardship, but this did not mean that they were discouraged and gave up on life. On the contrary, Adam's son Cain rose up and built a city. Many archaeological stories record the founding of cities which became closely tied to the establishment of a nation or people in the ancient world.

These cities were usually built along or near rivers or springs, and as time passed, they became focal points for trade, culture, and religious activity for the surrounding regions, eventually developing into political centres or city states.

By the time of Abraham, there were countless rich and powerful civilisations in the river valleys of Egypt and Mesopotamia. Walled cities and strongholds also arose to protect the settlers and those who farmed the surrounding country. Furthermore, nomadic tribes would travel from place to place in search of suitable grazing for their flocks.

Food Production

Following the lineage of Cain, Lamech's three sons Jabal, Jubal, and Tubal-Cain, contributed much to the prevailing society. Jabal is recorded as the forerunner of tent dwellers and cattle breeders; Jabal was the father of those who live in tents and raise livestock (Genesis 4:20).

Josephus (37–38/1987) stated that Jabal constructed tents and loved the life of a shepherd. He went on to say that "raising livestock was the first stage in animal domestication, and with the emergence of shepherds and cattle breeders, farmers would have grown grain crops, olive trees, and many other types of vegetation as food sources."

Musical Beginnings

Verse 21 of Genesis 4 shows that Jabal's brother, Jubal, *was the father of all who played stringed instruments and pipes.* As has been said, Jubal was not the inventor of music, but was the first person to build an instrument. Josephus (37–38/1987) further developed this idea when he stated that Jubal "exercised himself in music and invented the psaltery and harp." This is noteworthy, as it stresses the need for practice to become proficient in one's craft.

> From this Jubal, not improbably, came Jobel, the trumpet of jobel or jubilee; that large and loud musical instrument, used in proclaiming the liberty at the year of jubilee.

Note the connection with the Hebrew word *yobel* for ram's horn, which is played during the year of jubilee.

Ancient Metal Technology

The third brother, Tubal-Cain, *was a metal worker who forged all kinds of tools out of bronze and iron* (Genesis 4:22). Like his grandfather Cain, Tubal-Cain was given practical skills with which to adorn and enhance their dwellings and cities, supplying the many commodities available, like stones, rocks, gold and precious metals from the earth.

In these five verses, Genesis 4:17–22, the writer identified in embryo form the total sum of humankind activities derived from Cain. This included the building of cities, agricultural development, the rise of the arts, music, and metal work, all of which have remained throughout the centuries.

Literary Styles

In verses 23–24, the first lyric poem, known as 'The Song of the Sword', introduced a new literary element, the first epic poem. An epic poem, or simply an epic, is a poetic form which has been used by citizens throughout the centuries to extol famous people or situations.

Many nations throughout the world have their own epic sagas that consist of semi-historic and mythic tales, which have been passed on orally from generation to generation and are extant even today. They include Icelandic sagas, German sagas, and Spanish romanceros, together with Greek mythology, all of which inspired many literary giants and composers of the late Romantic Period.

Interest in these epic works was the inspiration of a new style of drama called fantasy writing. Wagner, one of the greatest composers of opera, based his epic music drama, *The Ring Cycle*, on Nordic and Germanic tales. English writers including C S Lewis and J R R Tolkien also successfully embraced the use of epic sagas as a means of telling spiritual truths.

Continuation of Divine Worship

Following the death of Abel, Adam's third son, Seth, continued the godly lineage, followed by Enoch and others, right through to Noah. However, as time passed, the gift of choice so lovingly given to Adam and Eve was abused, with humankind jeering at God, turning to every kind of wickedness. *Now the earth was corrupt in God's sight and was full of violence* (Genesis 6:11).

God's response to this conduct was to step in and destroy all that he had created. He implemented this by sending a raging torrent to earth, returning it to a watery chaos. Nonetheless, as always, God's love for his creation prevailed and he allowed one lone family, together with some animals, to enter the ark – that gargantuan boat which Noah built – and thus be saved. After the flood had receded, the first thing Noah did when he, his family, and the animals came out of the ark, was to build an altar to the Lord.

Noah's blood sacrifice, like Abel's offering, remained the central act of Israel's personal and corporate worship until the nihilation of Jerusalem in AD 70:

> Then Noah built an altar to the Lord … he sacrificed burnt offering on it.
> *(Genesis 8:20)*

God was so pleased with Noah's total obedience, that culminated with the sacrifice, that he vowed:

> Never again will I curse the ground because of humans, even though every inclination of the human heart is evil from childhood. Never again will I destroy all living creatures, as I have done.
> *(Genesis 8:21)*

The Lord continued:

> As long as the earth endures, seedtime and harvest, cold and heat, summer and winter, day and night will never cease.
> *(Genesis 8:22)*

He then blessed Noah and his sons, saying to them:

> Be fruitful and increase in number and fill the earth ... Everything that lives and moves about will be food for you. Just as I gave you the green plants, I now give you everything.
> *(Genesis 9:1–3)*

God's Covenant with His Chosen People

As described in the Pentateuch, God made three covenants with humankind. Each of these affirmed God's expectations of moral behaviour by all, together with immutable promises on his behalf.

The first promise was to Noah when God promised him he would never again send a flood to the earth:

> Then God said to Noah and to his sons with him: "I now establish my covenant with you and with your descendants after you and with every living creature...on earth."
> *(Genesis 9:8–10)*

This covenant was not given solely to Noah but included all humankind and all creation.

The second was his promise to Abram:

> On that day the Lord made a covenant with Abram and said, 'To your descendants I give this land.'
> *(Genesis 15:18).*

> Abram fell facedown, and God said to him, "As for me, this is my covenant with you: You will be a father of many nations. No longer will you be called Abram; your name will be Abraham, for I have made you a father of many nations.
> *(Genesis 17:3–5)*

The third promise summarises God's agreement with Moses on Mount Sinai, in the Book of the Covenant:

> Then he took the Book of the Covenant and read it to the people. They responded: 'We will do everything the Lord has said; we will obey.'
> *(Exodus 24:7)*

A covenant, a formal agreement between two parties, was common among nations in early times and covered all kinds of human relationships. It was a bond which united people in a mutual obligation, such as a marriage contract, or a business enterprise. The principal section of a covenant included stipulations which were agreed upon by both parties. As with the covenant between God and Moses, God made promises to people, and in return they needed to abide by God's laws.

The Rainbow

After the flood, the Lord repeated his covenant to Noah. This agreement included all of creation, emphasising the responsibility of every human being to care and nurture all the earth:

> God said, 'This is the sign of the covenant I am making between me and you and every living creature with you, a covenant for all generations to come: I have set my rainbow in the clouds, and it will be the sign of the covenant between me and the earth.'
> *(Genesis 9:12–13)*

The significance of the rainbow does not necessarily indicate that this was the first time a rainbow had been seen, but here the purpose of the sign is connected to the meaning attached to it.

Noachian (Noahide) Laws

When God declared he would not destroy the earth and all in it, according to the *Babylonian Talmud*, he reinforced the need for obedience of the laws he had given to Adam and Noah and the remaining descendants of Adam:

> Whenever the rainbow appears in the clouds, I will see it and remember the everlasting covenant between God and all living creatures of every kind on the earth.
> *(Genesis 2:16)*

The *Babylonian Talmud* recorded six commandments, prohibiting idolatry, murder, adultery, blasphemy, and robbery as well as a further command to set up courts of justice. After the flood, a seventh law was included, forbidding the eating of flesh cut from a living animal. Later these laws were named the Noachian Laws.

The Encyclopaedia Britannica (2019) cites that "Throughout the ages scholars have viewed the Noachian Laws as a link between Judaism and Christianity, as universal norms of ethical conduct, or as a basic concept in international law, or as a guarantee of fundamental human rights for all."

The covenant given to Noah unites all humanity under God's authority, both morally and spiritually. Therefore, from long before Moses until the end of time, each and every person is answerable to God. It never ceases to amaze me how much our Creator loves us by imparting to each of us a way of life that protects and enhances us in our daily existence.

The Lord reaffirms the worth of all living things by demanding an account for the life of another human being, because each person's heredity is from the Lord himself. *Whoever sheds human blood, by humans shall their blood be shed; for in the image of God has God made mankind* (Genesis 9:4–5). The *Reader's Digest Who's Who in the Bible* (1994), and

Ezekiel 14:20, name Noah, Daniel and Job as ancient Israel's three righteous men. Some commentators note that Ezekiel may have been referring to an earlier prophet named Daniel who may have been an ancient sage of the Syrian region. He is thought to have lived between Noah and Job and is also supposed to be the father-in-law of Enoch as mentioned in the *Book of Jubilees*.

Daniel is also known from extra biblical texts found at Ugarit, an ancient port city in northern Syria. Whoever Daniel actually was, it appears that during his lifetime he too was a 'God fearer' in those ancient times.

It was from the sons of Noah, through their lines of descent, that the world was repopulated after the flood:

> These are the clans of Noah's sons, according to their lines of descent, within their nations. From these nations spread out over the earth after the flood.
> *(Genesis 10:32)*

Tower of Babel

Human beings, the climax of creation, are superior to all else, accountable only to their Creator. At every stage of human experience whether good or bad they continue to work His purposes.

The Lion Handbook to the Bible (Millard, 2009) says: Human history is the outworking of God's plan. He is wholly responsible for the world and all that is in it, throughout all the people's lapses and self-will, throughout the centuries. God tempers his response to sin by using a blend of justice and mercy.

From clothing Adam and Eve, debarring Cain from human society, beyond the destruction of the flood and the scattering of the nations, there is always God's ultimate intention for humankind's wellbeing and blessing.

The story of the Tower of Babel was the next great lapse of humanity. The people reverted to grave wickedness, as they did prior to the flood, which resulted again in them turning away from God. This gargantuan event is an example of how whole nations can become full of arrogance, pride, and self-deceit. It stemmed from the idea that humans could ignore God's commands, and even have the ability to erect a temple that would reach heaven itself. Hence, God responded by confusing the people's languages and scattering them over all the earth.

As with so many events recorded in the Bible, archaeological evidence has been uncovered about this cataclysmic occasion. For example, bricks were used in construction: *let us make bricks, and burn them thoroughly* (Genesis 11:3). Cliff and Barbara Wilson (1990) endorsed the use of bricks: "One such article gives us a description of the early settlers living between the Rivers Euphrates and Tigris, beginning prior to the flood". They continued, "Genesis 11:2–3 is a thumbnail sketch of the early Sumerian civilization. Some of the recovered bricks had been heated to about 900 °F' (484 °C).

Another example of archaeological evidence is a copy of an early replica of King Ur-Nammu of Ur, showing him to be a faithful servant of the gods, with a basket of mud on his head as he helped to build a Ziggurat, a temple tower. This has been recorded as a meeting of judgement by the gods and is remarkedly close to the record in the Biblical account, in Genesis 11:7–8, which describes how the temple was destroyed, the people dispersed, and their language confused.

Conclusion

This was the last time God dealt with all of humanity *en masse*. From that time on, God ceased dealing with nations, instead choosing to work through righteous individuals who were found to be true to himself.

Abraham was the first of these men of faith, and from him rose a nation through whom all the world would be blessed.

The blessings include the Bible and later, through these, came the greatest event ever to occur in human history, the birth of His Son.

13. MESOPOTAMIA

The Country of Abraham

To understand the development of the Hebrew race both culturally and socially, and the background of this region and many other civilisations that influenced this race, necessitates careful study. This is because much of what the Hebrews experienced living and working with these civilisations, was integrated into the future development of the Hebrew nation and later, the world.

At the beginning of the fourth millennium, not long after the flood, the Sumerians who entered Eastern Mesopotamia became one of the greatest nations of that era. Going from strength to strength they redefined themselves by subjugating the lands around them. This created a culture of the highest order, prompting the Sumerians to become one of the most durable influences on world thought and development.

Internally, they had a complex system of government and a well-developed structure of commerce. They were also known to have invented cuneiform, one of the earliest forms of writing, which was commonly used for issuing receipts and making contracts and other documents.

Three thousand years of history were recorded in Sumer, and during this time the area had several distinctive names according to a particular period. These included Sumer, Akkad, Babylonia, Chaldea, and more recently Mesopotamia, known today as Iraq. To the north-west were Assyria and Northern Mesopotamia, to the south-west was Egypt.

Due to their advanced knowledge of architecture, the Mesopotamians and the Assyrians, together with some Akkadians and Babylonians, organised their society into city states, all of which had *ziggurats* (temples), palaces, and other two-storey dwellings made of brick. They also had many sophisticated, domestic inventions, such as water cisterns and drainage, which improved the lifestyles of their citizens. Each of these cities excelled in a different craft, like the guilds later formed in Europe. Ur, traditionally connected with Abram, was renowned for its skill in metallurgy.

The Sumerians built extensive roadways and trade routes which strategically included India and China and ended in Egypt. These routes were built to ensure the safety of the travellers transporting their wares from one place to another. This also meant that many ideas were transmitted from country to country.

Phillip J Cunningham (1992) describes these routes in detail, showing how they would eventually mean safe travel for Abraham's long journeys:

> The main road led from the cities along the Tigris and Euphrates, north and then west to the Mediterranean where at a crossroads, highways went north up the coast and south to Egypt. It will be in this scenario that a further link in the history of God that the chosen nation will be played out.

Although many people lived in urban environments, there were also wealthy pastoralists, and it appears Abraham's father Terah may have been one. Terah possibly lived outside the city, and if so, may have been kept informed about significant developments such as irrigation in agriculture. Furthermore, Abraham most likely was well-educated and would have participated in religious and city activities.

Mathematics, Astronomy, and Music

Early Sumerian life was structured around the temple, with religious and political authority being tightly integrated. These temples were also important places of learning, where priests, liturgists, mathematicians, musicians, and astrologers worked together resulting in many great scientific and mathematical discoveries.

It is also thought that the temple scribes were the men who invented cuneiform writing and composed many epics and poems which were used in later centuries. Through the study of their literary texts and tomb writing, we have discovered how they may have lived from day to day.

The Origin of Early Theory of Music

Astronomers and astrologers who studied the motion of the stars believed that the stars influenced men's destinies, creating a perfect harmony throughout the universe. Cuneiform sources reveal an orderly system of diatonic scales, which included tuning stringed instruments into alternating intervals of fifths and fourths.

The Mesopotamians were not the only ancient players in the advancement of music. Yehudi Menuhin (1977), noted that "ancient Chinese and Indians, as well as the Mesopotamians and Egyptians knew the consonant intervals of octave, fourth and fifth, and made them the starting point of various scale systems including ultimately our own". As the unity between these disciplines became stronger in Chaldean times, they influenced world thinking on many levels.

Worship Throughout Ancient Mesopotamia: 3rd and 4th Millennia BC

The ziggurats of the larger cities were dedicated to one or many gods. Ur and Haran were dedicated to the moon god Nanna (Semitic Sin or Su-en), and about a quarter of the city of Ur was used for worship of their gods.

A ziggurat named 'Hill of Heaven' stood on the top of a hill and was considered the dwelling place of the god Nanna. It was here that various rites and services went through a regular cycle in the natural course of the year. Rites included sacrifices to their gods together with liturgies both long and short. These services were led by the priests and musicians who performed daily.

One of the oldest religious concepts in the ancient near-east, was the belief in a great female deity – a universal mother of all life. A young god was associated with her who mostly appeared as her lover. So-called sacred sexual activities were consummated by temple priests and priestesses as part of these rites.

One such practice was that every woman was supposed to

offer herself at least once in her lifetime to the priests, although, if she was wealthy, she could arrange for a temple prostitute to take her place. Over two thousand male and female prostitutes converged on the city Ur at night. Even the archaeologists who discovered this practice reported that the degrading treatment of women was a great blot on the culture of Ur. Worship of the cosmic gods, heavenly and astral, was everywhere.

Until the beginning of the second millennium BC there were trained musicians in abundance. These included certain male musicians named royal servants who served in the temples and lived in colleges attached to these temples. Each college had a precentor who was not only the music director and chief singer but was also responsible for training the choirs and orchestras. The temple musicians who performed at religious ceremonies were involved with the royal orchestras of flute players and harpists and played at civil occasions.

Vocal and Instrumental Music

During this period, a single hymn or psalm was chanted in honour of one or more gods. Hymns and other liturgical music accompanied sacrifices, ritual purification, and festive occasions. The liturgies were often lamentations, and from the words which have survived, show highly organised poetical forms. The forms of their chants were possibly based on the poetical forms.

The techniques of temple chanting included that of response, alternative singing by the precentor and the choir, and antiphon, which alternated congregational singing and choir. Each poem had its proper chant and was considered to have an ethos or quality which made it suitable for communion with a chosen deity, which gave it some magical power.

These gods were propitiated by the proper use of the human voice and musical instruments. Although countless literary remains of what they sang or cantillated have come down to us in vast quantities, we have no way of knowing the actual sound produced.

Sumerian and Babylonian musicians were divided into casts of professions. Vocal and choral pieces were called Sem, and Sumerian chants were called Sir.

Ersemma Hymnology – Groups of Singers and Instrumentalists

- psalm or hymn set to a reedpipe
- the singers were divided into two categories:
- Nar – musicians who sang praises of the gods and kings
- Gala – those who sang laments.

Instruments of Mesopotamia

The most important instruments in Sumer were arched harps and large lyres – some almost as big as a man.

Other types of instruments unearthed include:

- **percussion** – cymbals, bells, tambourines
- **drums** – balag drums, lilis kettledrums, frame drums, footed drums, an hourglass drum
- **wind** – pipes, flutes, trumpets
- **sem** – a reed pipe, vertical end blown flute – one relief

shows a silver double pipe about nine inches long, and another pipe with four finger holes; a reed instrument was found in Ur

- **strings** – harps, lyres, and lutes (several casts were made and showed lyres with either ten or twelve strings)
- **zag-sal** – a cross-stringed, bow-shaped harp
- **miritu** – a smaller harp
- **zakkal** – an upright, vertical harp
- **eshirtu** – a ten-stringed, horizontal harp.

Eshirtu and algar were depicted on later Assyrian reliefs.

It is difficult to know who sang and played what, but it seems clear that the Cantillation (kalutu – chanting) would have been undertaken by precentors, called *sum* (gala), or *akkd* (kalu).

For the rest, there were instrumentalists called *zammer* who possibly sang with their instruments. Then there were other musicians called *naru*. This may have been a term that included both choristers and instrumentalists.

Around 1800 BC, the Babylonians became rulers for 540 years, and reached a high cultural level. The music of the temple services, which had previously consisted of a single hymn or psalm, were superseded by a complete liturgical service, combining several psalms or hymns with varied instrumental interludes.

Many of the poems had their own tunes and rubrics, such as, 'A Song to a Tune' and 'Thou Wilt Not Cast Down.' Some of these tunes and titles appear to have been incorporated into the Jewish repertoire, and in turn survived in the early English psalters. In this later period the temple appears to have added female singers, and processional movements to the ensemble.

Secular Music in the Life of Early Sumerians

Although only the priests and wealthy people would have been able to read, music was available to all, being transmitted orally from one generation to the next. From seals and plaques, we gather that, like any other community from the highest and greatest of society to the poor and those considered insignificant, music played an important role in their lives. For example, farmers who sang when sowing and harvesting, and shepherds who piped to their sheep and dogs.

The armies marched to the beat of drums, and later the Assyrians went to war with their instruments strapped to their bodies. In addition, women made music and danced accompanied by many instruments at feasts, military triumphs, burials, and other rites.

The vast amount of literature discovered by archaeologists includes a description of instruments, poems, and songs. One such poem was found on a clay cylinder relic, and described in script the use of music in the fabric of their lives:

> To fill with joy the temple court
> And chase the city's gloom away
> The heart to still, the passions calm
> Of weeping eyes, the tears to stay.

This poem, so full of normal human emotion which we continue to feel, could have been written today.

Anne Kilmer (2001) summed up the importance of these early civilisations in the development of music. "Mesopotamia is of singular importance to the history of music. This is partly because the first known theory texts are from Mesopotamia." Of greater importance than this is the fact that Mesopotamia is the first instance where evidence of musical activity is documented in all three categories of source material that bear witness to the ancient world.

Using contemporaneous material such as remains of instruments, images of music making and thousands of texts which refer to music and musicians, creates the possibility of forming a wholistic picture of musical culture.

Mesopotamia's Degradation

There is a saying that people never learn! This certainly was the case in the great nations that followed the Tower of Babel. It was not long after this catastrophic event that these nations of the world turned from the Creator God.

With this rejection, ancient polytheistic religions based on objects of nature abounded. The polytheists also created whole races of gods who, acting as humans, were recorded to have committed the same acts of unspeakable debauchery that their creators committed. These debased religious rites were still rampant in Greek and Roman times.

Later in this text, the divine structure of a temple and all its activities is discussed. The similarities between the Mesopotamian architecture, the ordination, clothes worn by the priests, and training and performance of musicians within the services and the sacrifices, will be evident. All these elements are inert and not evil elements in themselves, but like so many other human activities they were misused by those seeking a means of debasing humanity.

Paul makes this clear in Romans:

> The wrath of God is being revealed from heaven against all the godlessness and wickedness of people, who suppress the truth by their wickedness ... For since the creation of the world God's invisible qualities – his eternal power and divine nature – have been clearly seen ... so people are without excuse.
> *(Romans 1:18–20)*

Later Paul wrote:

> Although they claimed to be wise, they became fools ... They exchanged the truth about God for a lie and worshiped and served created things rather than the Creator – who is forever praised. Amen.
> *(Romans 1:22–25)*

Conclusion

Early nations such as Mesopotamia, together with Egypt, China and India, left an inheritance of discovery and knowledge, which paved the way for the those who came after, to explore and advance the many treasures both on the earth and in the heavens.

A metaphor which was used to show the dependence of modern thinkers on the progress of the past was recounted by John of Salisbury in the sixteenth century. This metaphor was originally given by his teacher Bernard of Chartres, who taught that truth is transferred to us through tradition (Parris, 2006).

> We are like dwarfs on the shoulders of giants, so that we can see more and further than they, because we are raised up on their giant size.

14. THE CALL OF ABRAHAM
The Beginning of the Hebrew Race

When the Bible recorded the narratives of Abraham, Isaac, and Jacob, readers might easily assume that they existed in quite primitive conditions; however, this couldn't be further from the truth. Archaeologists have discovered there was an evolving, somewhat complex, development of culture and technology, together with scientific research and application.

Abraham, Isaac, and Jacob are considered the patriarchs of the Bible. The broad meaning of the word patriarch is a social system whereby men hold primary positions in a society, such as political leadership, moral behaviour, social privilege, and control of property. A patriarchal system means that one person is given the responsibility of each group, including their livestock, guaranteeing their protection and maintenance throughout their lifetime. This style of leadership is still evident in many cultures throughout the world.

God's Change of Direction

In the early narratives of Genesis, from Adam and Eve through to Noah and the Tower of Babel, God is depicted as dealing with all humanity. Even when the Lord rescued individuals like Noah and his family, they were saved from a judgement that applied to all the world.

At this point, God formulated another plan, the call of

Abraham. God chose one man and his family upon whom he would bestow his special revelation, care, and promises. This divine message in Genesis simply recounts the story of the beginning of a family saga, which continued throughout the Bible, and is still present in some communities today.

Abraham's Lineage

The lineage of Abraham began with Shem, who was the ancestor of all the sons of Eber (Genesis 10:21). Flavius Josephus (1987) , in his book *The Antiquities of the Jews*, commented on the Hebrew name given to Abraham and his descendants. Josephus documented that it came from Heber/Eber, whom he believed was a forebearer originating from Noah to his son Shem.

Eber is considered to be one of the bearers of the monotheistic tradition, which he learned from his ancestors Shem and Noah, who then passed it on to his grandson Abraham. Eber was also connected to the Hebrew language which Abraham spoke and may have preceded the development of other languages used at the time.

The Bible begins the story of Abraham when he is a relatively old man. However, there are many indications regarding his upbringing; for example both Abraham and Terah were men of considerable wealth and prestige. As they were pastoralists they did not live in the big cities, and their wealth, like their livestock, was movable property. Nevertheless, they were still heirs of the great Sumerian culture of Ur.

Abraham's Youth

Abraham most likely would have been given an education worthy of his position in the community. Wilson and Wilson (1999) cited just how educated the Mesopotamians were, as a schoolhouse was uncovered at Ur dating from about Abraham's time. Similarly, an early form of the mathematical theorem named the Hypotenuse, known to be used in Mesopotamian times, was found on one of the early tablets (Wilson & Wilson, 1999).

In a modern version of this, we are told that in a right-angled triangle, the square on the hypotenuse equals the sum of the squares on the other two sides. Wilson and Wilson (1999) also observed that perhaps many students of Abraham's time wrestled with geometric principles, just as many high school students around the world continue to do today. Later, these calculations were revised and developed by the Greek astrologer Pythagoras, and are known today as Pythagoras theorem.

The knowledge we have today indicates that some modern writers think that the ancient peoples of the Bible were primitive and undeveloped. However, the opposite is true. The wealthy and educated would have been knowledgeable and highly skilled, a fact which has often surprised archaeologists. Furthermore, Abraham would have been brought up in a religious environment, as the two cities mentioned in the Bible, Ur and Haran, were centres of moon worship. The Bible points out in Joshua:

> Joshua said to all the people, 'This is what the LORD, the God of Israel, says: "Long ago your ancestors, including Terah the father of Abraham and Nahor, lived beyond the Euphrates River and worshiped other gods..." Now fear the LORD and serve him with all faithfulness. Throw away the gods your ancestors worshiped beyond the Euphrates River and in Egypt and serve the LORD.'
> *(Joshua 24:2, 14)*

Just when and how Abraham received the call of God is not recorded, but it would have meant leaving not only his roots but also worship in the splendorous temples which surrounded him. Instead, he followed the creator God, building simple monuments upon which a slain lamb may be sacrificed.

Abraham's journey begins:

> The LORD had said to Abram, "Go from your country, your people and your father's household to the land I will show you. I will make you into a great nation, and I will bless you; I will make your name great, and you will be a blessing. I will bless those who bless you, and whoever curses you I will curse; and all peoples on earth will be blessed through you." So, Abram went, as the LORD had told him.
> *(Genesis 12:1–4)*

English Old Testament scholar Harold Henry Rowley (1967) added:

Abraham began his pilgrimage of faith in response to a divine urge. His response to this urge was to obey. This pilgrimage would possibly have taken him along the ancient trade routes of the Fertile Crescent of Mesopotamia. The main road led from the cities along the Tigris and Euphrates, north then west to the Mediterranean where at the crossroads, a highway went south to Egypt.

Journeying would likely have been a traumatic experience in ancient times, and just how their day-to-day affairs were carried out is not overtly stated in the Scriptures. From other accounts, in extra Biblical writings, we know that the life of nomads involved various activities necessary for human existence. Abraham's family would certainly have been taught about God and had a general education. Practical skills would also have been passed from father to son and mother to daughter.

Oral Tradition

The story of the people of God in the Old Testament began with Abraham in Genesis 12, but oral tradition is as old as humanity itself. As nomads, it may be assumed that Abraham and his descendants may not have had implements to record detailed historical events, rather the stories would be related to the needs and interests of the hearers. The patriarchal stories would have been about God's promises of land, family rivalries, and longing for descendants. Others may have been in the form of teaching ways of life through moral songs and folk tales, with musical instruments which may have been brought from

Ur. There may also have been happy family times of caring and sharing.

Story-keeping was crucial to the Hebrews who later became the Israelites. They valued the gift of memory by developing various means to improve their own memories so that, throughout their history, they were able to recount God's faithful deeds to subsequent generations. God ordained that His people would remember His ways and pass this knowledge on to their children:

> Only be careful and watch yourselves closely so that you do not forget the things your eyes have seen or let them fade from your heart as long as you live. Teach them to your children and to their children after them.
> *(Deuteronomy 4:9)*

Like the Bedouins of today, Abraham lived a semi-nomadic life moving from pasture to pasture. During the famine in Canaan, he moved south to Egypt for a time, where he would have continued to absorb many cultural and social ideas, which he would have embraced in his early years in Ur. Furthermore, he would have encountered many other cultures from Sematic tribes during his wanderings. However, Abraham's faith in the eternal God, with its monotheistic concept (worship of a single Creator God), remained firm, not conforming to the idolatry of the surrounding nations.

Melchizedek

Meeting with Melchizedek is an interesting interlude in the life of Abraham. Melchizedek came to Abraham and offered bread and wine after the battle to save Abraham's nephew, Lot. In return, Abraham gave Melchizedek a tenth of the bounty he had won from the battle.

Melchizedek was the King of Salem (Jerusalem), and priest of the Most High God. David named Melchizedek in his prophetic Psalm:

> The LORD has sworn and will not change his mind:
> 'You are a priest forever, in the order of Melchizedek.'
> *(Psalm 110:4)*

> For it is declared: 'You are a priest forever, in the order of Melchizedek.'
> *(Hebrews 7:17)*

These verses describe Melchizedek as a sacred priest whose royal holiness transcended all human orders, having no beginning and no end, foreshadowing the divinity of Jesus. He appeared as a priest of the Most High God in a similar situation to Moses' father in-law Jethro. Melchizedek and Jethro had the office of priest long before the ordination of Aaron and his sons to the priestly roll, and long before the Levitical tribe was chosen for their official duties in temple worship:

> When Melchizedek met Abraham, Levi
> was still in the body of his ancestor.
> *(Hebrews 7:10)*

Both Melchizedek and Jethro were treated with reverence and respect by Abraham and Moses, as representing the Lord himself. By giving Melchizedek a tenth of the spoils of war, Abraham received a blessing from him. Similarly, Moses was blessed when he asked Jethro permission to return to Egypt to deliver his people from bondage. Later when Jethro brought Zipporah to Moses after hearing God's blessing for His chosen people, he responded by saying: *Now I know that the Lord is greater than all the gods* (Exodus 18:11).

Then, in his role as a priest, Jethro made a burnt offering and other sacrifices to God, and Aaron came with all the elders of Israel to eat a meal with Moses' father-in-law in the presence of God. Jethro also advised Moses on how to choose the judges and officers of the Israelites by testimonies of the people, before they were ordained by God (Josephus, 1987).

This manner of choosing bishops, presbyters, and deacons was later used in the Christian church. It is very encouraging to know that God had His ordained leaders in some communities throughout the world at this time. Both these priests Melchizedek and Jethro were working in their respective homes Salam and Midian as spiritual guides to the worship of Eternal God.

It would be a long time before Israel, as the chosen nation, would be able to set up a central place of worship with chosen personnel to oversee the spiritual leadership of the nation of Israel. This became a reminder of the time in Israel's later history when one of its prophets despaired of any anyone left in Israel who still served the Lord (1 Kings 19:18).

Continuation of the Patriarchs

Upon Abraham's death, Isaac, through a direct action of God, continued the line. He does not appear to have the inner strength and faith that was his father's, but he believed in the God as revealed to Abraham. God warned Isaac to remain on the land given to Abraham and He said to him:

> I will be with you and will bless you; for to you and your descendants I will give all these lands and fulfil the oath which I swore to Abraham your father.
> *(Genesis 26:2-3)*

Jacob, the last of the three great patriarchs, appeared an unlikely person to become a fulfillment of God's promise to the nation of Israel, since he was known by his actions as sly and sometimes fearful. According to the Old Testament and rabbinical tradition, these and other weaknesses clearly showed that it was divine will and not human intervention which established the Israelites in their promised land.

After he and his mother Rebekah deceived his father and received the patriarchal blessing, Jacob fled from Esau's wrath. On his journey Jacob experienced a heavenly vision during which God affirmed to him that he would receive the land which was given to Abraham and Isaac (Genesis 28:12–13). Here Jacob anointed the stone altar upon which his head had rested, thus dedicating it to God, and then named the place 'Bethel' or 'House of God' (Genesis 28:19).

On his return from Rebekah's homeland, Paddan Aram, Jacob then had a second spiritual experience. This time though, his struggle with the Lord was more sincere and tenacious (Genesis 32:24–26). Jacob proved this by his unwillingness to let go, choosing to fight on to receive the blessing, emerging from the struggle crippled, but a new man, together with a new name 'Israel' (Genesis 32:26–31).

Religion of the Patriarchs

As the patriarchs moved into Canaan, they worshipped at several different places which had spiritual significance – Shechem, Beersheba, Bethel, Hebron, and Mt Moriah. Worship during this period continued to be simple and individual, with its known forms of sacrifice and prayer. Abraham and the other patriarchs built their own altars, offered their own sacrifices, and received blessings from God. Their families and retainers were also included in the blessings.

Being nomadic, they did not stay in one place long enough to build a permanent shrine, nor were there any intermediaries, such as priests and musicians, to assist in and enhance their worship. Worship and life were closely related.

Music in Patriarchal Times

There is only one mention of music in the patriarchal period, and this was of a secular nature. It was when Laban reproached Jacob for stealing away without allowing him to celebrate his departure, and that of his daughters. This reference is a good example of how music was essential in the life of these early civilisations:

> Why did you run off secretly and deceive me?
> Why didn't you tell me, so I could send you away with joy
> and singing to the music of timbrels and harps?
> *(Genesis 31:27)*

The kinnor/cinnor (harp) is the only stringed instrument mentioned in the Pentateuch. It is possible that Laban being a Syrian, and not a Phoenician as often thought, may have been one of Abraham's relatives who lived in Haran. Therefore, the instruments described could possibly have been Sumerian and which, together with the religious icons and other familiar objects, may have belonged to Laban and his family.

Joseph

Joseph was the last great figure during the patriarchal period and was the second person to be called a Hebrew. As a young Hebrew boy, he demonstrated his courage to live up to the name Eber – Hebrew, meaning 'one is opposed' or 'on the other side'. Joseph openly worshipped the God of his ancestral fathers, when all others in Egypt were bowing the knee to celestial spheres including the sun, and many other gods.

Joseph was called by God from an early age to prepare the way for the Israelites to settle in Egypt, where they remained for four hundred years. After being sold by his brothers, Joseph spent his adult life in the courts of Egypt, which means he would have been highly educated in their arts and sciences.

To review the patriarchal period, Harold Rowley (1967) stated that Abraham and Joseph stood out as the two peaks among the patriarchs. It is observed of Abraham that, from a religious perspective, his life had a remarkable inner unity, made up of great trials and the development of personal faith. He is known as the father of the faithful and a friend of God.

Additionally, because the Lord was with Joseph, he had an inner strength based on his faith in God and holy living (Genesis 39:2). This inner strength was expressed in personal fellowship with his Maker, which led to righteousness. It would have been easy for Joseph to sin, yet he held firm regardless of the cost. He is forever an example to any young man or woman who may face similar temptations.

Due to Joseph's commitment to living righteously, and to the faith of his fathers, he was placed in a position to save his family from starvation; from being sold as a slave, he became the Pharaoh's Chief of Staff.

Drs Clifford and Barbara Wilson (1999) documented that "Egyptian Pharaohs were supposed to be the living manifestation of Ra the sun god. This actually is implicit in one of the titles that Pharaoh bestowed on Joseph, 'Father to the Gods'."

After Joseph revealed himself to his brothers, Genesis 45:8 states he changed his name to 'Father of Pharaoh':

> So then, it was not you who sent me here, but God.
> He made me father to Pharaoh, lord of his entire household and ruler of all Egypt.

He could not recognise the Pharaoh as a god, for only the true God could be acknowledged. This is an interesting pointer to his faith, which was the essence of Joseph's life.

Conclusion

Summary of the legacy given to future nations:
- From the call of Abraham to Moses (4000–1200 BC)
- Rise of the Sumerian civilisation in Eastern Mesopotamia
- Rise of civilisation along the Nile River
- First year of the Jewish calendar (3750 BC)
- Origin of cuneiform – the earliest form of writing (c. 3200 BC)
- Gilgamesh – legendary King of Uruk (c. 2750 BC) (Cunningham, 2020).

In the patriarchal narrative, worship is seen not in forms and ceremonies, but in a relationship between God and man.

15. BUILDING BRIDGES
Between Heaven and Earth

The unity of planet Earth with the heavens has been in the thoughts of people since the beginning of time. Views on astronomy were truly relevant due to the beauty of heaven as well as the influence of heaven on earth. Although it was obvious the sun brought light and warmth during the day, and the moon and stars gave off a lesser light during the night, both the sun and the moon indicated time, direction and seasons.

Many travellers, whether on land or sea, were guided by the sun and stars. Those who sailed the waters depended on knowledge of the stars to provide direction and awareness of clouds or a darkened sky. This navigation enabled travellers to be ready for any dramatic changes in weather patterns, such as storms, wind, rain or hail.

Travellers by sea and land were not the only people interested in the skies; notable learned men whose passion was to discover more about the heavens in relation to human life on earth were actively recording their findings. Although few resources were at their disposal, the early astronomers and astrologers made it possible for people to enjoy the sophisticated environment in which we now live.

In ancient times, wise men described the results of their studies of the heavenly hosts as 'constellations' or 'groups of stars'. Matthew Chapter 2, affirms the existence of wise men, also known as Magi, who most likely originated from Mesopotamia (now Turkey, Syria, Iraq and Kuwait). From the earliest time, these astrologers were popular leaders, and were recognised and respected for their great learning, including King Herod who listened with great concern to what they said:

> During the time of King Herod, Magi from the east came to Jerusalem and asked, 'Where is the one who has been born king of the Jews? We saw his star when it rose and have come to worship him.' When King Herod heard this, he was disturbed, and all Jerusalem with him.
> *(Matthew 2:1–3)*

It is speculated that the wise men's knowledge of Israel was based on the prophecies of the coming Messiah as told by the Jews and held in Babylonia thousands of years prior to the arrival of the Messiah. It is also speculated that being astrologers, it was possible that they recognised a new and unusual star or comet, which would have foretold the birth of Christ the King in Israel. Regardless of how the wise men arrived at this conclusion, Herod heeded their message.

Contribution of Job

References to the stars found in the book of Job are extremely important, as it is considered by many to be the oldest book in the Bible. Whether this is so, or whether it was written later is irrelevant, as it is a poem describing Job's dilemma.

It is believed that Job lived after the flood, which occurred about 180 years before the time of Abraham. Therefore, Job and Abraham could have been alive at the same time. Job was said to be a very wealthy man, who most likely was educated not only about the Lord, but in all the knowledge of the east.

God allowed Satan, the enemy, to test Job to see if he would remain true to him, even if he lost everything. Although at times Job had doubts, he remained true to his faith. This was verified when he declared to his friends the *profound nature of God's wisdom, and God's vast power* (Job 9:4). Job continued his acclamation of faith by proclaiming God's control of all heavens and earth, and his ability to *move mountains, stretch out the heavens ... and tread on the waves of the sea* (Job 9:5, 8).

James Warner Wallace (2018) observed in Job 38 that the Lord spoke to Job from out of a storm, and that God went on to name the four great constellations of stars as part of His creation. These stars and constellations are significant, as they were recorded several times in scripture, as well as in works of other authors who believed they had special influence in raising storms and tempests. Furthermore, God added another constellation, Mazzaroth, which is still relatively unknown (Job 38:32).

Pleiades of the East

In Job 38:31, after many questions about His eternal creation, God then questioned Job specifically about his knowledge of the stars, commencing with, *"Can you bind the chains of the Pleiades?" Pleiades* in Arabic means 'a knot of stars', that is, an open cluster of stars in the constellation of Taurus.

In his article *Is the Astronomy in the Book of Job Scientifically Consistent?*, Wallace (2018) enlightens further:

> [Pleiades] is known as the 'Seven Sisters' because it is a group of hundreds of stars formed from the same cosmic cloud and are bound to one another by a mutually gravitational attraction. Here God seems to be saying, 'Can you keep this heap of stars together?'

Orion

The Vulgate (2012) describes Orion in Job 38:31 as *'the shining stars'*. God also challenged Job in verse 39, with a question: *"Can you loosen Orion's belt?"* God was referring to the Belt of Orion which consisted of two stars, Alnilam and Mintaka and a one-star cluster Alnitak. Unlike the Pleiades clusters which shared a common trajectory, it is thought that in the course of time, Orion's Belt would be loosened, as God had told Job.

Arcturus: Great Bear of the Northern Hemisphere

This northern constellation is one of the greatest and brightest stars of the night, with a speed of flight at 413 km per second (257 miles per second). During the great age of antiquity, Arcturus was considered a single star; however, in 1971 astronomers discovered fifty-two other stars connected to it. In view of this, Poole (1962) proposed that God's question to Job, in Job 38:32, can be considered remarkably relevant: *"Can you bring forth the constellation in their seasons or lead out the Bear with its cubs?"*

Constellations of the South – Innermost Chambers of the South

Although Job lived in the northern hemisphere, he was cognisant with the stars and constellations located near the South Pole called the inner chambers. Most of the time they were hidden in these parts of the world, only rising to appear at the beginning of summer when they were thought to raise southerly winds and tempests (Poole, 1962).

Music of the Spheres

Musica Universalis – Harmony of the Skies

Musica universalis is an ancient concept which involved the proportions in the movements of celestial bodies – the sun, moon, and planets as a form of music. The source of *musica universalis* knowledge was shared by wise men, whose ideas can be traced back to between 3000 and 4000 BC, from many ancient civilisations, including China and India, Suma, Mesopotamia, Chaldea (now southern Iraq) and Egypt. These wise men expressed belief in a cosmic harmony pervading the universe and uniting the heavens with earth. Menuhin (1977) wrote that although these beliefs were modified and adapted to the specific cultures and religious mythologies of each of these nations, from earliest times there was a connection between the nations, and as these early civilisations developed, their beliefs became more sophisticated.

The wise men's scientific approach to life led them to consider the interconnectedness between music, mathematics, religion, and astronomy. This notion of interconnection was developed further as the wise men studied the basis of regular and rapid audible sound tones. These music tones resulted in atmospheric vibrations which were known by the ancient Egyptians as vibratory energies of the words of their gods, and as celestial energies of perfect harmony by the ancient Chinese.

Pythagoras (570–490 BC)

After studying ancient philosophical concepts of the temples of Mesopotamia and Egypt in the sixth century BC, the Greek philosopher and mathematician Pythagoras observed the proportions in the movements of sun, moon, and planets as emitting their unique hum or tone on their orbital revolution.

According to Pythagoras and many later philosophers, all nature is musical, and music illuminates the study of astronomy, while astronomy supplies a context for understanding music. Thus, it is through mathematics that nature can be known.

As with others, Pythagoras did not consider this music to be audible. Pythagoras' followers, the Pythagoreans, took this concept further, by calling these sounds 'tones', and so named them 'musica mundane', that is, the 'music of the spheres' or 'harmony of the spheres'. These ideas continued until the end of the Renaissance period when scientists described these movements as 'orbital resonance'.

Another discovery considered to have been made by

Pythagoras was that vibrations formed musical pitch. One way this became clear to Pythagoras was when he observed stringed instruments and found a precise relationship between the pitch of a musical note and the different lengths of the strings. This led him to claim the geometrical humming of strings and music in the spacing of spheres. Since Pythagoras did not record the results of his ideas, it is thought that much of what he claimed was documented by the Pythagoreans.

These ideas spread throughout the centuries as many scholars continued to question and advance his theories, specifically the music of the spheres.

The early Christians were enthusiastic about understanding God's intelligence and workmanship in His great cosmos. In the second century after Christ, Clement of Alexandria (Clemens, 325 AD/2010) a Greek theologian, philosopher, and Head of the Catechetical School of Alexandria, described the link between music and rhythm as fundamental to the concord between the heavens and earth. He claimed that "God's creative song ordered the universe concordantly and tuned the discord of elements in a harmonious arrangement, so that the entire cosmos might become a consonance through its agency."

Plato (424–348 BC)

Plato, an Ancient Greek philosopher who was considered to be the greatest scholar in the classical period, also regarded the proportions of the movement of celestial bodies in our hemisphere – the sun, moon and planets – as a form of music. In his writing he unites these celestial bodies and music together as twins. He developed this unity by proposing that "astronomy and music are twinned studies of sensual recognition – astronomy for the eyes, music for the ears, both requiring knowledge of numerical proportions" (McAleer, 2020).

Trivium

As Plato explained in his dialogue, three subjects of importance comprised the trivium, and were considered the lower division of the seven liberal arts (Oxford University Press, 1991). The trivium comprised:

- Grammar – teaching the mechanics of language to the student
- Logic – the mechanics of thought and analysis
- Rhetoric – the application of language in order to instruct and persuade the listener and reader.

These three subjects were together defined as the trivium in the Middle Ages. However, tradition considers they had become known in Ancient Greece. The writers of these works included Ptolemy, Cicero, Aristotle, Microbus and Boethius . Other works of literature from the Medieval and Renaissance periods were also filled with concepts of the music of the spheres and the planets.

Boethius (c. 480–525 AD)

A Roman statesman, scholar and Christian philosopher, Boethius became an important bridge between the ancient and medieval worlds. In his book *De Institutione Musica* (The

Principles of Music), Boethius described the Pythagorean unity of mathematics and music, uniting this with the concept of the relationship between music and society (Bower, 1966). Boethius once stated, "Music is part of us, and either ennobles or degrades our behaviour."

Quadrivium

Boethius observed a connection between music, mathematics, and astronomy, their impact on education, and the subsequent inclusion of music in the quadrivium – the medieval curriculum. Indeed, the quadrivium was used as a text at universities until the late eighteenth century. The quadrivium comprised of:

- Arithmetic
- Geometry
- Astronomy
- Music.

Together with the trivium, the quadrivium made up the seven liberal arts, which are still the basis for higher education today. Academic subjects such as literature, philosophy, and science have since been included.

Suzannah Clark (2005), co-editor of the article *Medieval Music and Renaissance Musical Culture*, described other theories of Boethius:

Conceptualising the harmony of the spheres in the Early Middle Ages, Boethius used popular concepts in dealing with his theories to encourage their use in human application. He succeeded in this as his books opened the door to new ideas and precepts by dividing the harmony of the spheres into three types:

- Musica mundane – music of the spheres and cosmic harmony among the stars, planets, seasons, and elements is unheard due to the lack of sensitivity in human ears
- Musica humana – the union of body and soul
- Musica instrumentalis – audible music including that of the voice as an instrument.

Boethius classified three types of musicians: those who perform, those who compose, and those who critique songs and performances (Rico, 2005). Around Boethius' era, the theorists and critics were thought to be the true musicians; however, the practising musician was not as respected.

John Williams Griffith II (2017) suggests that Boethius' *De Musica* applies to all art forms, and all creative artists are a conduit to portray beauty to the world rather than be a creator. Griffiths asserts that artists connect us to the arts and to each other to deepen our experience with reality.

Descartes, Copernicus, Kepler, Galileo, and Newton from the Renaissance period were all actively engaged in experimentation and discussions with like-minded people of their time, often at the expense of their reputation or their life (Brahma, 2017).

Nicolaus Copernicus (1473–1543)

Copernicus, a Polish mathematician and astronomer of the Renaissance period, contributed much to the scientific world by radically reforming the ideas of astronomy. He placed the sun at the centre of the universe with the planets orbiting around it. The idea was called heliocentric or a sun-centred system.

Two Greek philosophers in the fifth century AD, Philolaus and Hicetas, had separately considered that the earth was a sphere, revolving around a mystical fire. It appears that these concepts were not established. Later, however, when Copernicus developed his ideas on astronomy, they were considered so controversial that in 1616 the church vehemently labelled them heretical, to the point of banning his work –, *De Revolutionibus Orbium Coelestium, Libri VI'* (*The six books on The Revolutions of the Celestial Spheres*) (Copernicus, 1999). Nevertheless, Copernicus was considered an initiator of the Scientific Revolution.

Galileo Galilei (1564–642)

Throughout his lifetime and also today, Galileo has been considered a hero of science due to his discoveries of Jupiter's moons, the mountains on the moon, and heliocentrism. Heliocentrism is the solar system whereby the earth and other bodies revolve around the sun at the centre of the universe.

Most people at that time believed the earth was the centre of the universe, and the sun and planets revolved around the earth. It's not surprising then that Galileo was met with great opposition (*Galileo Galilei*, 2017).

Galileo and the Church

Galileo was considered a hero by many of his contemporaries. *The Stanford Encyclopedia of Philosophy* (2021) notes that "Galileo was and is seen as the 'hero' of modern science ... his major claim to fame probably came from his trial by the Catholic Inquisition and his purported role as heroic rational, modern man in the subsequent history of the warfare between science and religion", yet the church of the time condemned Galileo as a heretic.

His first misdemeanour was called the Galileo Affair (Finocchiaro 1615/1989). After publishing *Dialogues Concerning the Two Chief World Systems*, Galileo was ordered to Rome to be examined by the Holy Office of the Inquisition.

He was also charged with the support and endorsement of the work of Copernicus and his sun-centred system. He was tried by the inquisition and, like Copernicus, was named a heretic and sentenced to house-arrest.

This did not deter his search for truth, which is evident in a letter he wrote in 1615 to Castelli and which was transformed into the *Letter to the Grand Duchess Christina*. In this letter he argued that, of course, the Bible was an inspired text, yet two truths could not contradict one another. So, in cases where it was known that science had achieved a true result, the Bible ought to be interpreted in such a way that makes it compatible with this truth.

The Bible, he argued, was a historical document written for common people at a historical time, and it had to be written in language that would make sense to them and lead them towards the true religion.

The Stanford Encyclopedia of Philosophy (Galileo Galilei, 2017):

> Throughout all this troublesome time he maintained his faith and his work there was no conflict between his faith and his scientific discoveries. Galileo believed that God reveals himself every moment in the majesty of nature's laws. Science is the lens through which to see those laws, and science, he declared, can only advance.

Johannes Kepler (1571–1630)

Kepler, a man filled with passion and determination, was a key figure of the scientific revolution of the seventeenth century, and became known for his laws on planetary motions. He was strong in his defence of Copernicus' ideas that differed from the ideas of older astronomers, displaying his support by writing a book in 1621 called *Epitome of Copernican Astronomy* (translated by Charles Glenn Wallis).

Kepler is most remembered for his three planetary laws:
- circular motion principles for satellites
- mathematics of satellite motion
- energy relationship for satellites.

It is the adoption of the ideas of Pythagoras and his work in 1619 *Harmonica Mundi* (translated 'Harmony of the Worlds') which are of interest here. He continued using the concept 'musica universalis' or 'music of the spheres'. The central theme of this was the importance of the harmonies in the universal order.

Kepler felt harmony displayed geometrical proportions which were reflected everywhere, the archetypes of universal order, from which the planetary laws, the harmonies of music, the drift of the weather, and the fortunes of man are derived. He adds, "These geometrical ratios are the pure harmonies which guided God in the work of Creation".

Another of Kepler's theories was that the music of the spheres was a continuous and everchanging tone.

Kepler was a devout Lutheran, with God and the Creation as the centre of his being, but like many other men of God, he suffered for his faith. As a Lutheran he was under suspicion by Rome, and from other Lutherans, due to his friendly relations with the Calvinists at his university.

After 1530, with the reformation under Martin Luther in Germany, Protestantism took roots in many other parts of Europe, which led to open hostility, culminating with a conflict known as the Thirty Years War (1618–1648). In reality, this was a struggle for the balance of power between the Austrian Habsburgs and the German princes. Kepler lived during these troublesome times, and his book was published near the start of the The Thirty Years War (1619).

During this time, a great plague was raging which killed not only many of his friends but also many of his family members. The loss of life was so great that Germany's population was reduced by a third at the end of the century.

But his faith in God and his beliefs never wavered and he ended his book with a triumphal note of praise:

In vain does the god of war growl, snarl, roar, and try to interrupt with bombards, trumpets, and this his whole tarantantarum . Let us despise the barbaric neighing which echoes through these noble lands and awaken our understanding and longing for harmonies.

Isaac Newton (1643–1727)

Newton, another renowned figure of the scientific revolution in the seventeenth century, came up with the theory of the Law of Gravitation of 1687. This proposed that an object in space will remain at rest, or in constant motion , unless acted upon by a force. The force can be anything that slows or quickens an object – a push, gravity, friction, or resistance. The sum of the forces is equal to the mass and multiplied by acceleration.

Put anywhere in the universe, at a fixed distance apart, at once the gravitational force between them is known. His ideas paved the way for many scientists to develop their notions into the twenty-first century.

Newton, having been influenced by three Italian books by Kepler: *Astronomia Nova, Harmonices Mundi*, and *Epitome of Copernican*, became extremely interested in how music theory was such an important component to the understanding of light. He was interested in the parallel between the colour spectrum and the musical scale, by noting that the seven notes of the scale, before returning to the octave are similar to the colours of the rainbow – red, orange, yellow, green, blue, and violet, in addition to indigo which made up the seventh note. He also, through his interest in Pythagoras' views on musical consonance, together with his own views on gravitation, reinterpreted the ancient notion of the harmony of the spheres.

Newton, of great faith and knowledge of God and his universe, believed like David of old, that the word of God was the source of truth and light. He penned these words:

> We account the Scriptures of God to be the most sublime philosophy. I find more sure marks of authenticity in the Bible than in any profane history whatsoever.

Moving through the nineteenth and twentieth centuries and into the twenty-first century, though we have become aware of the endless galaxies of stars, countless light years away, and though nations can send manned rockets into space and see them return safely, scientists still have no definitive theory to show how a universe without boundaries can exist.

Albert Einstein (1879–1955)

Einstein contributed much to the nineteenth and twentieth centuries; in fact, it is considered that the world was changed forever when he recognised problems in Newton's 'Law of Gravitation' theory (Siegel, 2019). It inspired him to formulate his new concept, 'General Relativity'.

In 1905, when Einstein was twenty-six years old, he published five papers in the *Annalen der Physik*. The third paper of this series was the special theory of relativity, which quietly amalgamated space, time, and matter into one fundamental unit (Snow, 1967). This supplied solutions to some of the greatest puzzles of nineteenth century theoretical physics.

Einstein, as an accomplished musician, was interested in the concept of musical vibrations in the heavens. Personally, music was an important part of his existence. Among his many quotes it is recorded that he wrote:

> If I were not a physicist, I would probably have been a musician, I live my daydreams in music. I see my life in terms of music.

In another quote, he expressed a desire for his science to be unified, harmonious, expressed simply, and to convey a sense of beauty of form (Viney, 2018).

Steven Hawking (1942–2018)

Although, over the past hundred years, there have been great strides achieved in research of the heavens, Bishop George Appleton (1987) wrote:

> Even Stephen Hawking, one of the greatest scientists of today, after much research, was only able to come up with another speculative idea called Infinite Time.

Geyser (1999) commented on this:

> Hawking who distinguishes between his mathematical time which has no beginning, and real time in which we live which has a beginning, admitted that if there was

a beginning, then it is reasonable to assume there was a creator.

Another area of research which Steven Hawking continued in the twenty-first century, was his black hole theory. He helped to give more solid mathematical backing to the black hole, enlarging on Einstein's prediction in his theory of relativity.

Planetary Sciences (2019) quoted Steven Hawking as stating that "the theory of general relativity predicts that sufficiently compact mass can deform space time to form a black hole".

Earlier observations had revealed a prodigious amount of light and heat, created by black holes. Professor Andrew Fabian and fellow research colleagues from the Institute of Astronomy at the University of Cambridge have now detected that in addition to light and heat, the galactic black holes have sound (University of Cambridge, 2022). In musical terms the pitch of a sound generated by a black hole converts into the note B-flat, fifty-seven octaves below middle C. To date, this is the deepest note detected from an object in the universe and is not heard by humans. Steve Allen, a co-investigator with Fabian, adds, these sound waves may be the key in figuring out how the galaxy clusters, the largest structures of the universe, grow.

Hawking, as with many other theoretical physicists, believed that the instrumental 'string theory' of Pythagoras, is a fundamental way of describing the makeup of the universe. Auditory culture is thereby extended to the smallest particles and the largest galaxies (Samuel, 2009). This agrees with Stephen Hawking's concept of auditory culture in which he proclaimed that sound is everywhere from tiny particles to large galaxies.

These ideas and experiments made by so many throughout the ages, continue to unite music with the heavenly spheres.

Conclusion

Here we have discovered countless men and women who in their time on earth had the courage to advance their theories of the heavens in connection with our own planet, so that others who came later could evaluate and build upon these concepts.

Although we humans came into the world with little knowledge of ourselves and our surroundings, through sourcing the gifts God has given us, we are capable of discovering anew, great and wonderful things which can be embraced and expanded upon during our time on earth.

One of the greatest of these scientists, Robert Sapolsky (2004), was quoted saying:

> I love science, and it pains me to think that so many are terrified of the subject or feel that choosing science means you cannot also choose compassion, or the art, or be awed by nature. Science is not meant to cure us of mystery, but to reinvent and reinvigorate it.

16. LIFE IN EGYPT

A Time of Hardship and Development as a Nation

The timespan from the call of Abraham to the death of Moses is approximately four hundred years. Little of this Egyptian period from the death of Joseph to Moses is known except that which is written briefly in Exodus, Chapter 1. The focal point of the narrative during those centuries was the enslavement of the Hebrew people. Yet, prior to their enslavement, they would have been immersed into the Egyptian life and culture.

Although as a young man, Joseph would not have clearly understood the reason for being sent to Egypt, as time progressed, he would have become aware of God's plan for his life. Later, when he was promoted to Pharoah's chief of staff in Egypt, Joseph became instrumental in bringing his own family to Egypt so that they could escape a famine which ravaged both Egypt and Canaan.

When the Hebrews arrived in Egypt, they were a small group of nomadic shepherds with little knowledge of the logistics of nation development and housing construction. By the time of Moses, they had developed into an extremely large nation. As documented in Exodus 1:7, "*the Israelites were exceedingly fruitful; they multiplied greatly, increased in numbers and became so numerous that the land was filled with them.*"

Historical Background – Egyptian Music and Culture

From the end of the Patriarchal Age, 1550 BC, when Israel entered Palestine, Egypt dominated the ancient world, and Palestine lay within its empire. Prior to this time, as with Mesopotamia, Egypt had reached a high level of civilisation, illustrated by the skilled workmanship in all they created. Archaeologists have dug up countless drawings of fine furniture, crafted copper utensils, carved alabaster, exquisitely made gold ornaments, and hand-painted pottery, all of which showed the level of cultural attainment.

The Egyptians were also skilful architects and builders. Pharaoh Amenhotep III (1403–1364 BC), also known as Amenophis III, engaged in a building program which, although accomplished for his own glorification, contributed to making Egypt a magnificent place. Later, under the reign of his son Pharaoh Amenophis IV (1364–1317 BC), further building developments took place. Amenhotep IV, also known as Amenophis IV, changed his name to Akhenaten – meaning Splendour of Aten, the sun god – and built himself a new capital city, Akenten at Tell el-Amarna.

As with the Sumerians, and later the Hebrews, music infiltrated the Egyptian culture, from the Pharaoh's court with its many festivities, banquets, and processions, to the working classes. Court musicians held privileged positions from the earliest times, when male musicians sang, played instruments, and danced. Prior to 1500 BC, Mesopotamian and Syrian people, with other monarchs from Semitic lands, sent dancing girls to Egypt. These girls became part of the harems, thus changing the style of local dance.

Daily life was often painted with fine accuracy on the tombs of courtiers. Sometimes paintings in homes featured the homeowner reclining, the family seated playing harps, women dancing, and servants singing.

Gods of Egypt

The Egyptian pharaohs were thought to be the living manifestation of Ra the sun god. This is implicit in one of the titles, 'father to the gods'. The pharaohs were also priest kings, and so their court music was naturally linked with temple tradition.

Additional Egyptian gods were ruled by the chief goddess Isis, who was initially an obscure goddess, but, together with her consort Osiris, became two of the most important deities of ancient Egypt.

Even though they worshipped the sun god, like many other ancient nations, Egypt was polytheistic, and the inventors of arts and crafts created many gods for the worshippers. The use of an artisan to make idols is one of the accusations made by the Lord to Israel through his prophet Hosea:

> Now they sin more and more; they make idols for themselves from their silver, cleverly fashioned images, all of them the work of craftsmen.
> *(Hosea 13:2)*

Many of these artisans, the Egyptian Ptah, the Greek Hephaestus, and the Germanic Vulcan, were also worshipped by mortals.

Many of the Canaanite gods identified with local deities such as Baal (Seth), Hauron (Horus), Reshef (Astarte) creating a substantial influence on the religious life of the Egyptians and being adopted into the Egyptian pantheon. In turn, the Hebrews were influenced by Egyptian culture and religion.

For centuries the Hebrews lived in Goshen, an area in the Nile Delta, where worship of Horus the Bull cult was widespread. In Egypt, the bull or calf was a symbol of fertility and physical strength, while in nearby Canaan, the bull or calf was the animal of Baal, the god of storm, fertility, and vegetation. The golden calf made by Aaron and the children of Israel at Sinai, portrayed in their minds this god-bull Horus which worship was practised at Goshen (Exodus 32).

Temples and Worship in Egypt

Egyptians were great builders of palaces and cities as well as temples. These edifices were used daily for the enactment of solemn ceremonials, together with many other yearly rituals such as priests chanting praises and supplications to their many gods.

As music played a dominant role in worship in the temples, one of the main purposes for this was music education. The Egyptians took music education very seriously, with state laws controlling all music and the arts, with certain songs taught to the children by law.

As musical abilities were considered to be hereditary, young males of certain priestly families were trained from an early age to become temple singers and instrumentalists.

Often the instruments themselves were dedicated to one of their many gods. For example, bells and flutes were dedicated to Osiris, the lyre to Thoth, and the sistra to Isis. Music education of a particular class was later adopted by the Levitical family for worship in the tabernacle and the temple.

Part of the education of all priests would have included vocal training. This was a crucial element in their training as they believed the human voice was able to contact the powers of the invisible world.

Some songs used in ceremonies still survive. One set, 'Songs of Isis and Nephthys', was part of the funeral hieratic papyrus of Nesi Amsu. It was sung by two virgins in the temple of Osiris during an annual five-day festival to celebrate the sowing season in the fourth month. Unfortunately, chants were transmitted orally, so no music has passed on in notation form (Ancient Egyptian Texts, 2020).

From the Middle Kingdom, when the Hebrews were slaves in Egypt, several pieces of literature are extant today, one in particular is the 'Song of the Harper'. This genre of ancient Egyptian music was performed at funerary pageants, and it was found in tomb inscriptions, being placed beside a portrait of a man playing a harp or flute (Ancient Egypt Online, 2010).

The harper's job was to sing of the bliss of the deceased who now resided with Osiris – the God of Egyptians, together with rejoicing songs. Thirteen heretic songs, twelve of which have been found in Thebes, question the afterlife and urged people to enjoy their current life. These songs appear to be written in poetic prose which parallel those found in the Book of Ecclesiastes.

Egyptian Music and Notations

There is a rich body of documentation about ancient Egyptian musicians, instruments, statuary, hieroglyphic instruction and song texts. Mostly they are concerned with religious music – texts to hymns and psalms, together with statues of music-making gods. However, they give no hint to actual musical tunes which may have accompanied the songs. One example is a figure found in Egypt (c. 4000 BC) depicting two women playing instruments and a third woman clapping her hands (Menuhin, 1977).

Although no notations representing sounds and pitches have been discovered, it has always been assumed that people of such intelligence and artistic creativity would have had a music system. This idea has been reinforced when, from the third millennium BC, during temple ceremonies, there have appeared many depictions of chironomy – people giving direction in hand signs to singers and instrumentalists.

It is thought that some of the finger positions of performers in bas-reliefs (sculpture), demonstrate how they played their instruments, and may have also matched pitches and scale degrees. The use of chironomy has continued throughout the centuries and remains today as the Gregorian chants in Christian liturgical music. This style of hand instruction is the start of the use of conductors and music directors.

A number of ideas have been expressed regarding the use of chironomy. For example, pictures showing two signs being given simultaneously have been said to indicate the essence of polyphony even in the earliest times. Another concept is an approximate scale being derived from studying the hands on the strings of harps and other instruments. Furthermore, A, F, E, C, B, appear to indicate that Egyptian music may have been woven around the pentatonic scale. According to Josephus (1987), lyres which set the time were enharmonic, that is, they could change their keys from, say C to C sharp.

Musical instruments typical of the Old and Middle Kingdoms are:

Strings:
- arched harps
- angle harps
- ayres
- auloi
- long-necked lutes

Wind:
- clarinets – single reed
- oboes – double reed
- pipes – Hebrew halil

Brass:
- trumpets – copper, bronze (straight trumpet played by soldiers)
- flutes – vertical, transverse

Percussion:

- clappers – metal, bone, ivory
- sistras (rattles) – V-shaped frame with metal strips (cult instrument)
- cymbals – metal with little knobs
- tambourines – small hand drum with metal rings around the edge, round or rectangular.

Families of flutes, auloi, trumpets, harps, clarinets and sistras have all been depicted in tombs. Other representations have shown ensembles of musicians playing several types of instruments, along with singers, chironomists, and often dancers.

Enormous orchestras of that time were often described on papyri by Egyptians as having over six hundred harps, sistras, flutes and tambourines. Even accounting for some exaggeration on behalf of recordists over the size of temples at the time, it would have taken these large numbers to make an effective sound. Ancient Egyptian music, in its stable tradition, constituted a continuous progression from the Old, Middle, and New Kingdoms, down to Greek and Roman times.

As we have looked at the culture and religion of the dominant nations of the world prior to the Hebrews, it is obvious that there was a deep unvarying need for worship, as each nation appears to have a similar pattern of structure and style of worship. This style of worship involved a form of hierarchy, including priesthood and other personnel who attended to the running of all functions from daily services to religious festivals which marked seasonal events.

Included in this hierarchy were trained artisans, who created beautifully designed furnishings for the temples, and skilled musicians who were employed to assist in the services. All these elements in themselves would have been in the hearts of the nations of Mesopotamia and Egypt, together with countless other nations not mentioned in the Bible.

These inanimate objects were used to enhance the practice of worship and were pivotal in inpiring the worshippers. The Hebrews, however, set up worship centres to glorify God, choosing to serve the Creator, not the created.

Conclusion

As we move forward, we will note how the Hebrews were blessed in their worship of the Lord but suffered greatly when they followed the surrounding nations.

When God gave instructions to Moses on how to build the tabernacle, the institution and the portrayal of so many elements
can be compared with those of other nations. Therefore, it can be concluded that it was not the elements that were evil, but their misuse by the worshippers.

17. MOSES AND THE EXODUS

God's Mighty Rescue of His People

The Exodus is considered the most important event in the history of Israel, and was accompanied by much rejoicing and excitement, as well as apprehension. It was planned by God himself who gave instructions to Moses to prepare him for such a massive event. Pharaoh's subsequent attempt to recapture his slaves was thwarted by God's pillars of cloud and fire and the subsequent swamping of Pharaoh's chariots when the Red Sea parted, clearing the way for the Israelites' passage, but not the Egyptians' (Exodus 13–14).

Period of Hebrew Captivity and the Exodus

Due to their slavery and the heavy burdens placed upon them during the latter part of their time in Egypt, it is unlikely the Hebrews would have had much opportunity to be formally educated. However, they would have continued to receive oral instruction, clinging to the faith of their forefathers – belief in God, history, and traditions which were passed on from generation to generation.

This strong belief in their God and their calling would possibly have been strengthened by their bondage. It is reasonable to consider that a formal type of epic poetry, which includes songs, rhythm, and repetition, may have been used, as this style makes memorising easier to remember than for prose.

This form of memorising poetry continued throughout Israel's history.

The Hebrews may have orally taught their children singing and how to play instruments; however, as there was no audio recording possible, the Hebrews, together with the other nations at that time, could not pass on an exact record of how their instruments would have sounded. In addition, the women appeared to have been talented in singing, dancing, and playing the toph, an Egyptian instrument named the timbrel (Exodus 15:20-21). This is indicated when the women joined Moses in praise and gratitude to the Lord when they were released from their bondage in Egypt. Even at this early stage of Moses' leadership he reveals himself as a fine poet and songwriter, skills which were possibly developed during this time in Egypt.

Moses' Education

Egypt may have been primitive when compared with the amount of learning which has evolved since that time; however, its written language was extensive and sophisticated. Historical records of this have been preserved on the walls and monuments of their cities, as well as on papyrus.

Any lack of formal education did not apply to Moses, as he, like so many of the great reformers whom God chose throughout the centuries, was well-equipped for the task. From the beginning of his life, Moses was placed in situations where he would have been given the highest standards of education and training. It began when Pharaoh's daughter rescued a

Hebrew baby, giving him the name Moses, meaning 'drawn out' in Hebrew, describing the manner of his salvation.

Moses' preparation for ministry began with his birth mother who may have been highly aware that her son was destined for greatness. Moses' birth mother, Jochebed, was given the task of caring for him during his formative years, and most likely would have taught him about God and His chosen people, enlightening him of his lineage.

Later, Moses was reared in Pharaoh's court as Pharaoh's daughter's son, and with this went all the privileges of royalty. His education would have included reading and writing, mathematics, science, including astronomy, weaponry, horsemanship and music.

Acts 7:22 tells us that in Stephen's speech to the Sanhedrin he affirmed that *Moses was educated in all the wisdom of the Egyptians and was powerful in speech and action*, which implies that Moses received an education befitting an Egyptian prince.

As a young man in his glory days in the court of Pharaoh, Moses would have been a great fighter and orator, with plenty of confidence in himself and his natural abilities. Without such discipline and training, he may not have been able to cope physically or mentally with the eventual task God had for him.

The 'Faith Hall of Fame' (Hebrews 11:23–25) tells us of Moses' parents who, despite the risk of betrayal, had the faith and courage to hide him for three months after his birth to save his life. Later, Moses' own faith was recorded, acknowledging him as remaining true to God by refusing to be acknowledged as the son of Pharaoh's daughter, choosing instead to be mistreated along with the people of God.

As Clifford and Barbara Wilson (1999) studied Pharaoh's daughter, Princess Hatshepsut, they concluded that she was the only female to become a Pharaoh in her own right. By retrieving Moses from the Nile River, she became his stepmother, realistically affording Moses to be much closer to becoming a Pharaoh than he may have realised (Wilson & Wilson, 1999).

Moses had many lessons to learn before he was equipped to fulfil the great commission entrusted to him. As an adult he did not forget his Hebrew origins, and at forty years of age he slew an Egyptian who was beating a Hebrew. When he realised his crime was discovered, he fled to the land of Midian in the Sinai desert, east of the Gulf of Suez, where he resided with the priest Jethro and married Jethro's daughter Zipporah (Exodus 2:11–21).

It is thought that the Midianites were descendants of Abraham through his second wife Keturah and were relatives of Moses' mother. If this is so, then like Jacob, Moses fled to relatives who were most likely believers in Creator God.

Later the Lord chose a Midianite sacred place, called the 'Mountain of God', where he revealed himself and his plan for deliverance of the Israelites. Thus, after being brought up in the lap of luxury during those early years, Moses became a humble shepherd:

> Now Moses was a very humble man, more humble than anyone else on the face of the earth.
> *(Numbers 12:3)*

Present day Christians can be encouraged by Moses' experience. It appears that before Moses fled from Egypt, he was undeniably a gifted speaker, powerful in both speech and action (Acts 7:22). Through a lack of confidence, this attribute appeared to have become lost during this period of his life. The hesitancy in his speech is understandable after spending forty years in the wilderness with only the animals for company. This lack of opportunity to have dialogue with others would have made any great orator unsure of their ability.

> Moses said to the Lord, 'Pardon your servant, Lord. I have never been eloquent, neither in the past nor since you have spoken to your servant. I am slow of speech and tongue.'
> (Exodus 4:10)

Like Moses, many people consider themselves invincible, only to fail to succeed in their quest to achieve great things for God. However, in God's economy, it is not so much relying on the strength of our own human giftedness; rather, it is simply what God has for us to do.

Moses' lack of confidence in his own oratory remained with him all his life, but it is amazing to realise how much he achieved for his God in obedience and humility. He might not have preached great sermons, but he was prepared and called to continue the drama of Creator God. Moses was used by God to make a safe path for every human being including the Hebrews, by reforming and enlarging God's holy rules and regulations which give life to all.

The writer of the book of Hebrews cites another act of faithfulness on Moses' part; the first Feast of Israel (Leviticus 23). It continued year by year and still exists among Jewish worshippers even today:

> By faith he kept the Passover and the application of blood, so that the destroyer of the firstborn would not touch the firstborn of Israel.
> *(Hebrews 11:28)*

Hebrew's Departure from Egypt

First Passover – Slaying the Paschal lamb

The Lord spoke and gave to Moses instructions for the Passover. These instructions were given during the three days of darkness to fully prepare Israel for the grand finale of life in Egypt. The Passover feast began on the evening of the fourteenth day of Abib (March/April) later called Nissan by divine decree, becoming the first year of the Jewish calendar (3750 BC) and marking out Israel's life as a nation.

> This is a day you are to commemorate; for the generations to come you shall celebrate it as a festival to the Lord – a lasting ordinance.
> *(Exodus 12:14)*

This Passover was so important to His chosen people that the Lord gave Moses every detail, including the suitability of the animal, when to kill it, what to do with its blood, and how to cook it. The Lord also ordained the preparation for the meal and the disposal of the leftovers.

The lamb not only provided a substantial meal for the arduous journey ahead, but the Hebrews were also directed to use hyssop to brush the lamb's blood on the sides and lintel of the door of each house, so the angel of death would see the blood and pass over. Therefore, this meal was a memorial of the Hebrew's protection from the angel of death which slew the firstborn children of the Egyptians, as well as freeing the Hebrews from their Egyptian bondage.

Feast of Unleavened Bread

On the fifteenth day of Nissan, they were instructed to remove yeast from their homes, bake unleavened bread for their journey and continue eating it until the twenty-first day of Nissan. The Feast of Unleavened Bread became the first of the eight appointed times of the Lord, which included the Sabbath. Seven periods in the Hebrew years were set apart as celebrations based on the sacrificial altar and worship of God, not just banquet feasting.

Alfred Edersheim (1874/1994) noted:

> While great prominence is given to the historical bearing of the Passover, the Feast of Unleavened Bread celebrated the one grand event which underlays the whole history of Israel and marked alike their miraculous deliverance from destruction and bondage and the commencement of their existence as a nation.

Commemorating the Hebrew exodus and the eating of unleavened bread for seven days, together with a warning against eating bread with leaven, ensured their bread would not become mouldy. From the very beginning, non-Israelites were included in the nation's religious festivals providing that the males were circumcised.

> A foreigner residing among you who wants to celebrate the Lord's Passover must have all the males in his household circumcised, then he may take part like one born in the land.
> (Exodus 12:48)

This regulation is reminiscent of the baptism often used in Christian churches as a requirement to be observed prior to receiving communion.

God also instructed the Israelites to take articles of silver and gold, as well as clothing from the Egyptians, so they did not leave empty-handed. Many of these items were later used in the construction of the tabernacle (Exodus 3:21–22). A note at the end of Chapter 1, Book 15 of Josephus (1987) states that God ordered the Jews to demand these gifts as pay and reward during their long bitter slavery in Egypt, as an atonement for the lives of the Egyptians and as the condition of the Jews' departure.

The Lord's instructions were also recorded in Genesis 23:14–17 and in Deuteronomy 16:8–12.

Celebratory Song and Dance

When the Israelites made their escape from Egypt, such a momentous occasion was expressed by the natural reactions of singing and rejoicing (Reader's Digest Association, 1994). The first song of the Lord was composed and sung by Moses, and Miriam joined in with the other women who played their timbrels and danced and sang the refrain:

> I will sing to the Lord, for he is highly exalted.
> Both horse and driver he has hurled into the sea.
> *(Exodus 15:1)*

This song in the book of Exodus introduced a new dimension of worship – community praise as one voice to Yahweh. Miriam and the women also played tambourines, which were considered to have been a 'toph', also called a 'tabret'; a small hand drum of Egyptian origin. In the Bible, toph is translated from the Hebrew nine times as a timbrel, and eight times as a tabret. The toph was round or oblong in shape with metal rings around the edge. Moses' song of victory set a pattern which was later used to mark national times of rejoicing.

A similar event was held to celebrate David and Saul's return as victors after the defeat against Goliath and the Philistines, with the women singing and playing the toph. Prior to these expressions of joyous communal worship, praise to God in some traditional communities such as Yemen and other early settlements had a similar style of victorious celebration. Today, some of these groups continue to be led by the personal acts of faith and worship of the Patriarchs, similar to Moses. The Lord abundantly blessed their households due to their devotion to Him.

Josephus (1987) wrote: These Hebrews having escaped the danger they were... employed in singing of hymns, and in mirth. Moses also composed a song unto God, containing his praises, and a thanksgiving for his kindness, in hexameter verse.

Hexameter is the oldest form of Greek and Latin poetry. Each line of verse in the hexameter contains three feet of dactyls (rhythmic units). In this poetry, a foot (a unit of division of rhythm) with one strong or long syllable is followed by two unstressed (not strong) or short syllables. There is a similarity between hexameters and the English iambic pentameter found in English versification.

Virgil (7019 BC) wrote his famous epic poem 'Aeneid' in dactylic hexameter. The editor of Josephus (1987) remarked:

> It is obvious that Josephus was familiar with the works of the Greek and Latin poets, as he speaks of several sorts of that meter or measure, both here and elsewhere.

Moses' Song of Deliverance

> I will sing to the Lord, for he has triumphed gloriously;
> He has hurled both horse and rider into the sea.
> The LORD is my strength and my song; he has given me
> victory. This is my God, and I will praise him –
> My father's God, and I will exalt him!
> The Lord is a warrior; Yahweh is his name!
> *(Exodus 15:1–3)*

The theme of the song is glory to the Lord and thanking him for the victory won over the Egyptians. Moses declared that the Lord was the source of his strength, and the architect of his deliverance and preservation. Because of this victory, God is the object of worship and praise with the divine name Yahweh repeated ten times.

The first four stanzas, verses 1–5, 6–8, and 9–10, recall the story of deliverance, verses 12–16 describe the miracle at the Red Sea, with verse 15 retelling the story of deliverance. Other poetic styles were used in this song, such as similes: verse 5, *they sank to the depths like a stone;* verse 8, *the surging waters stood firm like a wall;* verse 10, *they sank like lead in the mighty waters;* verse 16, *they will be as still as a stone,* which marks the conclusion of the first four stanzas.

Moses' song in verse 17 anticipates the future approach to and conquest of Canaan:

You will bring them in and plant them on your own mountain
    The place, O Lord, reserved for your own dwelling
    The sanctuary, O Lord, that your hands have established.

Moses concluded his song in verse 18 with one of our great acclamations of faith which has continued to resound throughout history even to the present time:

    The Lord will reign forever and ever!

Verse 19 then summarises the events which occasioned the song. Miriam and the other women who followed her in singing, dancing and playing instruments, concluded the song by repeating the first chorus:

    Sing to the Lord, for he is highly exalted. Both the horse
        and driver he has hurled into the sea.
                (Exodus 15:21)

The Israelites continued their journey passing from place to place until they came to Arnon on the border of Moab and the Amorites. Here Moses, and possibly the Israelites, recalled an excerpt from *The Book of the Wars of the Lord*, one of the several books no longer extant, which are, however, mentioned in the Old Testament. This book may have reminded them of the small desert town Beer, meaning 'water', where there was a well:

> That is why the Book of the Wars of the Lord says '...
> Waheb [Zahab] in Suphah and the ravines, the Arnon
> and the slopes of the ravines that lead to the settlement
> of Ar and lie along the border of Moab.'
> *(Numbers 21:14)*

This is an interesting and personal experience for the Israelites to be led of God and finding themselves on the right path. By this time, they needed water, and so the Lord guided them to a place where the much-needed water was available. From there they continued to Beer and the well where the Lord said to Moses:

> 'Gather the people together and I will give them water.'
> Then Israel sang this song: Spring up, O well!
> Sing about it, about the well that the princes dug
> That the nobles of the people sank
> The nobles with sceptres and staffs.
> *(Numbers 21:16–17)*

During their journeys to the promised land, this song, referring to a particular situation, was part of a time-honoured ritual of which they were familiar and continued to use as the tribe approached waterholes. Andrew Wilson-Dickson (2003) noted: "The study of musical cultures across the world suggests that remote and isolated settlements may have preserved musical traditions intact forever."

Wilson-Dickson also quoted the writer Bertram Thomas

(1892–1950), who earlier last century wrote a description of the morning of a long desert journey across South Arabia: "As we were arriving, the Bedawin moved at a sharp pace, chanting the water chants. These sounds were known as Bedouin musical shouts."

A fragment of an ancient poem or song preserved in the book of Numbers, describes the responses of Moses and the people when the Ark of the Covenant, a symbol of the presence of God, was taken up to continue their journey:

> Whenever the ark set out, Moses said,
> 'Rise up, O Lord! May your enemies be scattered
> May your foes flee before you.'
> Whenever it came to rest, he said,
> 'Return, O Lord, to the countless thousands of Israel.'
> *(Numbers 10:35–36)*

The cloud of the Lord was over them by day when they set out from camp, and a fire protected them by night. Until this point in their journey, the Hebrews appeared to be thankful for their release from slavery and used every opportunity to praise God with joyous sound.

It is interesting to note the various types of songs and instruments used at this time do not appear to be the babblings of ignorant people, but people who maintained their self-respect, regardless of the trials they suffered for so many years.

This celebration was not part of an organised worship service in a temple built for the occasion, but a spontaneous act of joy and praise to God for His mighty works. It was one of the many examples showing how worship of the Lord permeated the very fabric of life in Israel. This bond between the physical and spiritual was evident in the lives of all people known in surrounding regions at the time. Later in history, we discover a similar relationship between God and His people in Christian countries during medieval times.

Conclusion

The Israelites' obedience to the Lord became the foundation of the first two of their holy festivals, the Feast of Unleavened Bread and the Passover, through which, by continuing these festivals year by year, they were ever reminded of their salvation from death and the commencement of their life as a nation. From here, their journey continued on until they reached Mount Sinai, where a further revelation of the Lord and His holiness would be disclosed.

Rejoicing with music became the Hebrew's first community celebration of praise to the Lord.

18. DEVELOPMENT OF BEHAVIOUR AND WORSHIP
Ethical and Ritual

The Bible states that the sons of Jacob travelled to Egypt and continued to live there for over four hundred years before being led by Moses to Mount Sinai. Moses' main challenge was to weld a company of slaves into a nation whose bond of unity was their devotion to God, and to encourage their obedience to the high ideals set before them.

After travelling through the desert for nearly three months, the Hebrews arrived at Mount Sinai, which became a significant place. It was here that the Lord, because of His past faithfulness and evidence of his continuing mercy, established His covenant with Israel.

At this time, he set out the terms of the agreement, which included the basic principles that would govern the lives of the Israelites. These terms of agreement began with respect and honour shown to God himself, followed by social laws, which would cement their relationships with one another.

In earlier chapters, we considered prior covenants between God and His chosen people, noting that most covenants were bonds which united people in mutual obligations, similar to a marriage contract or a business enterprise. However, God's covenants were distinct as they were entirely one-sided with the initiative coming from God himself. Similar documents of one-sided covenants resembling the Moses covenant have been discovered from the era of the Mount Sinai covenant.

In 1945, an Old Testament scholar George E Mendenhall (1916–2016) realised that one such treaty, the Hittite Suzerainty treaty, had the same pattern as the account of the treaty or covenant which God made with Israel. Mendenhall considered the significance of this pattern in the Hittite Suzerainty treaty and showed that it coincided date-wise with the Hebrew text, possibly about 1200 BC (Feder, 2014).

The Hittite treaty told of a Suzerain (king) who sanctioned the Hittite (vassal king) to continue in his position by accepting certain conditions which were imposed upon him and his people. Both the king and citizens were compelled to pledge their loyalty in return. A comparison between this later covenant between the Lord and Israel and the Hittite contracts, reveals this similarity.

Feder (2014) undertook to clarify these similarities by exploring the meaning of the term covenant which existed between the Lord and His people. Feder and others found five components which met the Suzerain conditions:

1. Historical Preamble

The first nineteen chapters of Exodus describe the Israelites' redemption and their exodus from Egypt, with God reminding them that He brought them out of the land of Egypt, the house of bondage. The similarities continue as God identifies himself as the Suzerain:

> I am the Lord your God, who brought you out of Egypt,
> out of the land of slavery.
> *(Exodus 20:2)*

He did not identify himself merely as Creator God, but also as the Lord who provided blessings upon the Israelites and continues the blessing on all humanity. In exchange for these blessings, the Lord expected the people, compared to the Hittites, to be loyal and in submission to His will.

2. Terms of the Pact

After the historical preamble, the Hittite Suzerainty contracts generally detailed the conditions of the pact by the Suzerain on his vassals, and then expected them to reciprocate in an expression of loyalty. On Mount Sinai, details of the pact were given to Moses as a written document confirming the relationship between God and the Israelites. After reinforcing His salvation of the Israelites from Egypt, God's first commandment stressed that believing in any other deity is false, and not only false but invalidates the contract between God and the Israelites.

3. Placing the Contract in the Temple

Another element of the Hittite Suzerain contracts which paralleled the covenant was demonstrated when the Hittite contracts were placed in their temple. A copy of the Lord's Covenant was engraved on two tablets and placed in the Ark of the Covenant in the tabernacle, which became the Tabernacle of Testimony (Exodus 25:16, 21; Numbers 1:50). Later the Scroll was placed in the temple:

> Put in the ark the tablets of the covenant law,
> which I will give you.
> *(Exodus 25:16)*

4. Witnesses to the Covenant

In the time of Moses, many so-called 'witnesses' were included in the contracts between nations. These were often celestial beings and deities from heaven or from the natural world, such as earth, rivers, or mountains. However, the Lord not only assumed the role of the Suzerain king, but he also appointed himself as the one and only witness. Joshua Berman (2006) asserts that the Bible makes it clear that the tablets of the covenant are symbolic proof of the relationship between humans and God.

5. Blessings and Curses

The Hittite contracts generally concluded with the gods bestowing favours upon the vassal in exchange for his continued loyalty, or else the threat of misfortunes which would come upon the vassal if he were to disobey the contract. This concept was replicated when the Lord gave a similar list of blessings and curses to his people (Deuteronomy 28).

King Nebuchadnezzar the Great used the Suzerain style of contract when he installed Zedekiah as the vassal king of Judea. He then warned King Zedekiah to be loyal and obey him. The

Lord also told Zedekiah, through Jeremiah, to remain as he was, warning him if he disobeyed, he would be destroyed.

Sometime later Zedekiah supported some minor kings against Nebuchadnezzar and suffered the consequences:

> They killed the sons of Zedekiah before his eyes.
> Then they put out his eyes, bound him with bronze shackles and took him to Babylon.
> *(2 Kings 25:7)*

The covenant made by God to the Israelites strongly demanded that no treaties were to be made between the Israelites and their neighbours (Leviticus 34:15). Unfortunately, this was one law the Israelites wantonly ignored, and eventually resulted in the Israelites becoming captives and slaves to the neighbouring nations.

Some may consider the Hittite Suzerainty treaties irrelevant to our current consideration of this final Old Testament covenant between God and His people, which would in time embrace the whole world. Rather than be irrelevant, like many blessings which have been given to humanity, using a manmade treaty was especially important to ratify the relationship between the Lord and His people.

Prior to the theophany at Mount Sinai, Israel had been a group of slaves without any loyalty to Egypt, or any sign of God's requirements on their part to please him. The Israelites would have been aware of the Hittite Suzerain treaty, as any agreement between persons or nations was essential so all could live in harmony with each other. Where there is no strong or righteous person to govern, then anarchy is close at hand.

A close relationship with God has always been necessary for Israelite worship, for showcasing His continuing love for His Creation. The Lord, in knowing humanity better than they knew themselves, created in an immutable code as a basis of their lives, keeping them safe from so much that could destroy them. Like the Hittite Suzerain contract, the Lord further expanded the laws, warning them if they broke these laws, they would suffer dire results. Moses declared:

> Moses summoned all Israel and said: 'Hear, Israel,
> the decrees and laws I declare in your hearing today.
> Learn them and be sure to follow them.
> The Lord our God made a covenant with us at Horeb.
> It was not with our ancestors that the Lord made this covenant, but with us, with all of us who are alive here today.
> *(Deuteronomy 5:1–3)*

Ethical Requirements

Prior to Moses, Noah had received partial ethical standards of human behaviour which contained several rules for all humanity, regardless of ethnicity, colour, or belief. God showed that He was intimately interested in the world and its inhabitants and was not remote from humankind.

Whilst on Mount Sinai, Moses received a final covenant of corresponding laws of behaviour. It began with the Ten Commandments which Moses obtained from the hand of the

Lord and were passed on to the Israelites to learn and obey. Due to God's holiness, the Ten Commandments were not chosen by the Israelites as their regular standard of worship but by the Lord himself. Any choices made by people, like that of Cain who sought to appease the Lord on his own terms, was unacceptable.

Decalogue

The word decalogue does not occur in the Bible; however, the ten words were derived from the Greek language as found in Exodus 34:28 and Deuteronomy 10:4. The decalogue is a declaration of ethical monotheism – one God as confirmed in the first commandment, immediately followed by the second commandment:

> You shall have no other gods before me.
> You shall not make for yourselves an image
> in the form of anything in heaven above
> or on the earth beneath or in the waters below.
> *(Exodus 20:3–4)*

The Ten Commandments formed the moral basis upon which worship of Yahweh was achieved. It lifted the worship of Yahweh to a loftier plane than that of the surrounding nations who dictated their own patterns of behaviour and worship. The Canaanites, who surrounded the Israelites, were a prime example of a godless society based on human logic and desires.

The Ten Commandments – towards whom are they directed?

Directed to God	Conduct towards others
Devotion to Yahweh	Honour of parents
Absence from idolatry	Prohibiting Murder
Honouring the name of Yahweh	Prohibiting Adultery
Observance of the Sabbath	Prohibiting Theft
	Prohibiting False witness
	No envy

God revealed to Moses not only the Ten Commandments but also many other related laws based on holiness and justice, which were to be observed in the lives of the Israelites. Before permitting any ritualistic patterns of worship, the Israelites were to first seek God's holiness as the core of their existence:

> Be holy because I, the Lord your God, am holy.
> *(Leviticus 19:1)*

Peter endorsed this command in his letter when in Rome: Just as he who is called is holy, so be holy in all you do,

> for it is written: 'Be holy because I am holy.'
> *(1 Peter 1:15–16)*

This injunction was, and still is, for Jews and Christians alike. Jesus confirmed the Commandments were as relevant to all future believers when he replied to the rich young man's enquiry about how he could gain eternal life, by repeating five of the ten commandments, then adding: *'Love your neighbour as yourself'* (Matthew 19:16–19). On another occasion, the Pharisees challenged Jesus by asking him which was the greatest commandment in the law. Jesus responded with:

> This is the first and greatest commandment:
> Love the Lord your God with all your heart and with all your soul and with all your mind... and the second is like it:
> Love your neighbour as yourself. All the laws and prophets hang on these two commandments.
> *(Matthew 22:34–40)*

Throughout history, the decalogue has been a summary of God's laws and standards of behaviour, central to a Christian life of reverence and worship. All who strive to embrace these commandments will find holiness reflected in their own lives, revealing itself in practical concern for people who are disadvantaged or facing hardship, together with a desire to embrace justice, honesty, and fair dealing for all.

Rowley (1967) summed up the importance of the Ten Commandments when he wrote:

Worship is thus conceived as communion, not simply symbolized in the eating of a meal after part of the animal eaten had been offered on the altar, but in expressing itself in prayer. It should, moreover, be realised that obedience in the fulfillment of the Ten Commandments is also the service of God and therefore worship, for in Hebrew, service and worship are expressed by a common word (additionally, the same word can mean work).

Caring for the Land – Jubilee

Concern was also expressed by the Lord for good stewardship of the land. This included that one in every seven years the land should lie fallow, with an additional year of fallow every fifty years (Leviticus 25:1–13).

Israel's Response to Yahweh

One of the most inspiring Biblical passages is the description of Moses communing with the Lord on Mount Sinai, reminding Moses of his wondrous salvation and freedom, and with the subsequent humble response by the Israelites:

> Then Moses went up to God, and the Lord called to him from the mountain and said, 'This is ... what you are to tell the people of Israel: 'You have seen what I did to Egypt...

> Now if you obey me fully... You will be my treasured possession... You will be for me a kingdom of priests and a holy nation'... So, Moses went back... and set before them the words the Lord had commanded him to speak. The people all responded together, "We will do everything the Lord has said."
> *(Exodus 19:3–8)*

Three promises which particularly expressed God's love and generosity to His chosen people were that they would be:
- his treasured possession
- a kingdom of priests
- a holy nation.

With memories of the Red Sea rescue still resounding in their hearts and minds, the people's response to the covenant was unanimous and joyful in agreement. The covenant was formally sealed by a special sacrifice of young bulls. Moses then divided the blood and sprinkled one half on an altar and the other half on the people. By doing this he united the Lord and His people, the Israelites. Moses then declared:

> This is the blood of the covenant that the Lord has made with you in accordance with all these words.
> *(Exodus 24:8)*

Although this declaration was used to sanction the agreement between the Lord and the budding nation of Israel, it has continued to be spoken by priests and ministers, Sunday by

Sunday during the Eucharist, reminding believers of the death of Christ who became the Lamb of God for our eternal salvation.

Ritual Requirements

Having listed the acceptable terms of behaviour from His people, God gave Moses the instructions for true worship. The ritual requirements did not conflict with the decalogue, but together they formed two parts of the whole – holiness of life and obedience to the Lord in ritual. Each demanded the exclusive worship of Yahweh, forbidding images, and adhering to the observance of the Sabbath.

As we have moved through this text and witnessed the results of the Israelites as they turned from the Lord, we learned that the first element to cease from their lives was their holy worship! As indicated earlier, individual sacrifices were the acceptable type of worship. This personal worship continued until the development of the Hebrews into the nation of Israel.

From here on, we will consider God's instructions on how the Israelites were expected to conduct their corporate worship and become a witness to Himself to surrounding nations. The focus of the ritual decalogue remained Yahweh-centred, but the bond between God and His people was extended to thirteen rules, to include all the activities necessary to accommodate the agricultural conditions, which later would be required.

The first three ritual laws are God-centred, like those demands of the ethical laws:

- exclusive worship of Yahweh
- images are forbidden
- observance of the Sabbath.

Further instructions defined the ritualistic acts of worship relevant to the national festivals:

- three times a year all males were to appear before the Lord and bring Him an offering
- offering of the blood of the sacrifice with unleavened bread
- no Passover festival sacrifices were to be left until morning
- the finest of the first fruits of the soil were to be brought to the house of the Lord
- cooking of a young goat in its mother's milk was forbidden
- celebration of the Passover
- celebration of the Feast of Unleavened Bread
- celebration of the Festival of Weeks with the first fruits of the wheat harvest
- celebration of the Festival of Tabernacles (Ingathering) at the end of the year
- other ritual requirements – the first offspring of every womb belonged to God.

Israel's Relapse into Sin

Just six weeks after making their solemn covenant with God, while Moses was on Mount Sinai receiving the Ten Commandments from the hand of the Lord, the people back at base camp were becoming restless, and demanded that Aaron fashion an idol in the shape of a golden bull or calf:

> The people gathered around Aaron and said, 'Come, make us gods who will go before us ...' Aaron answered them, 'Take off your gold earrings ... and bring them to me.' ... He took what they handed him and made it into an idol cast in the shape of a calf ... Aaron and the priests then said, 'Israel, these are your gods, who brought you out of Egypt.' When Aaron saw this ... he announced, 'Tomorrow there will be a festival to the Lord.'
> *(Exodus 32:1–5)*

This was Israel's first rejection of God's holiness and a return to the orgiastic practices of those surrounding nations, whom the Lord abhorred. These practices incited the people to throw off those God-given inhibitions and behavioural patterns which would have normally restrained them, resulting in sensual dances, singing, and feasting, far from the concept of the kind of worship God was preparing for His people.

In this instance, the Israelites reverted to the fertility rites connected with the Horus cult of Goshen. This meant a shift in emphasis from righteousness, justice, and high moral standards to a purely material consideration which ended in the basest immorality and social degradation, resulting in shame and death.

Joshua heard the noise and warned Moses about the sound of battle in the camp. However, Moses knew his wayward people a little better, and replied to Joshua, saying:

> It is not the sound of victory, it is not the sound of defeat;
> It is the sound of singing that I hear.
> *(Exodus 32:18)*

Moses was shocked that the people could disregard God and His promises and horrified by their return to their old ways so quickly. He responded drastically by *throwing the tablets out of his hands, breaking them to pieces at the foot of the mountain* (Geneses 32:19).

As written in the introduction to *The Daily Bible* (LaGard Smith, 1984):

> Abraham's descendants chosen to reverse the failure of Adam had now also failed! However, God remained committed to his people and his plan.

It appears that Aaron lacked the piety and strength of character that was necessary in his leadership role. His response to the people brought dire results, which should have been a warning to future generations, but to no avail! After the death of Joshua, the people continued to embrace the worship of the Canaanite idols. The Book of Judges can be summed up in just two verses:

> In those days Israel had no king; everyone did as they saw fit. Everyone did what is right in his own eyes.
> *(Judges 17:6; 21:25)*

Conclusion

Unfortunately, the Israelites proved time and time again that as a nation, they did not possess the nobility of spirit which was evident in Abraham. However, God did not set His love upon them or choose them because they were more numerous than other nations, but simply because He loved them.

> Not for thy righteousness or the uprightness of your heart...
> for you are a stiff-necked people.
> *Deuteronomy 9:5-6*

One commentator writes:

> The most significant things that are taught about God's character are deeply stamped on the Bible as a whole, and they all stem from Israel's experience of God in the period of the Exodus.
> *(Source unknown)*

19. THE TABERNACLE

God Dwelling Among His People

The Tent of Meeting

Prior to the construction of the tabernacle, a tent of meeting was set up outside the Israelite camp to provide a place for people to enquire of the Lord (Exodus 33:7). This was to meet him either for private prayer, devotion and official business, or judicial matters:

> The Lord said to Moses: 'Bring me seventy of Israel's elders who are known to you as leaders and officials among the people. Have them come to the tent of meeting, that they may stand there with you.'
> *(Numbers 11:16)*

Significance of the Tabernacle

Having received the decalogue and other laws on moral and ethical behaviour from the Lord, Moses was given the blueprint details for the construction of the tabernacle together with the articles necessary for their daily services. The requirements of ritual laws stemmed from the need for people to live holy lives by worshipping according to the instructions ordained by their creator:

> Then have them make a sanctuary for me, and I will dwell among them. Make this tabernacle and all its furnishings exactly like the pattern I will show you.
> *(Exodus 25:8–9)*

> See that you make them according to the pattern shown to you on the mountain.
> *(Exodus 25:40)*

The primary place of worship recorded in the Old Testament after the temple, was the tabernacle. Situated centrally in the Israelites' camp, the tabernacle was used for sacrificial offerings, corporate praise and worship in the form of psalms and prayers. It was led by the chosen family of priests and Levites.

The tabernacle meant much more to the Israelites than just a place for communal worship. In the construction of the tabernacle, God reinforced His love for the people by affirming the first part of the covenant promise: *I will take you as my own people, and I will be your God* (Exodus 6:7). The tabernacle also represented the climax and completion of God's purpose that God would dwell among them, and was colloquially referred to as 'God in residence' (Exodus 25:8; 29:46).

The evidence symbolising God's holy presence among His people was the cloud of the Lord which covered the tabernacle by day and a fire which was in the cloud surrounding it by night:

> Whenever the people saw the pillar of cloud standing at the entrance to the tent, they all stood and worshiped, each at the entrance to their tent. The Lord would speak

to Moses face to face, as one speaks to a friend.
(Exodus 33:10-11)

It is thought that the tabernacle, although fragile, stayed with the Israelites from the commencement of the wilderness journey at Mount Sinai until Solomon built his temple.

Conversely, all other nations throughout the earth devised their own ways of worship, which included many gods and goddesses whose actions followed the wickedness of their inventers. The people then added to these deities other natural elements such as the sun, moon, trees, and beasts. To accommodate these idols, these other nations built magnificent structures, often placing them in the centre of their cities. No matter how great and glorious the edifices were, without acknowledgement of the Lord of all creation and following His holy laws, manmade worship centres were unacceptable to God then, as they still are today.

Symbolism and Imagery

The Bible narrative from Genesis to Revelation contains symbolism and imagery much like the tabernacle and its accruements which became a verbal picture book full of shapes, patterns, and meaningful ideas (InterVarsity Press, 1998). These concepts can help us experience a deeper level of understanding of the Lord and His rituals used in worship.

If we are willing to permit our imagination to wander through this Holy Place, take the time to reflect on significant items, together with the priestly acts performed on behalf of the people. Then these rituals will make sense.

Construction of the Tabernacle

The tabernacle was built as a tripartite and took six months to build. The architectural design was not unique, as it was used for early Egyptian Ziggurats, together with Canaanite temples (as found in Ugarit Shechem), which meant that the Hebrews were familiar with this style.

Every part of the building was strategically planned by God, including several kinds of curtains and coverings used to overlay the whole structure. The first layer was one of fine linen woven in threads of blue, purple, and scarlet, embroidered with figures of cherubim. Upon this was placed a curtain of goats' hair, followed by rams' skins dyed red, and finally a protective cover of badgers' skins was added.

It is interesting to note that these materials woven in the collage of colours symbolised many aspects of Israel's spiritual experience. Purple for the kingship of the Lord, blue for heaven, and scarlet the blood of the sacrificial lambs that were ever a reminder of the salvation of humankind.

Although the importance of the tabernacle and its symbolism belonged to the Hebrews of that time, the significance behind the symbolism is eternal because it represents the only time God intervened and gave instructions as to how He expected His people to approach Him and construct His Holy Place on earth. These concepts and structures remained as guidelines to many churches throughout the centuries as they planned and built similar places of worship.

The Outer Court

Bronze Basin

The first piece of furniture in the outer court was a bronze basin and stand which was situated between the altar and the tabernacle. This was used by Aaron and his priestly sons who assisted him to wash before entering the tent. In the Laws of Moses, there was a close relationship between cleanliness and godliness. This cleanliness was paramount for Aaron the High Priest, as he ministered in the tabernacle. Prior to entering the Holy of Holies on the Day of Atonement, Aaron used the bronze basin to bathe his entire body, so he was personally pure and acceptable to God.

Bronze Altar

The second most prominent Biblical image for worship and religious adherence was the bronze altar. It represented all sacrifices which consisted of the blood of animals from Cain and Abel until the death of the Lord Jesus Christ. John the Baptist, in his role of presenting Christ to the world, exclaimed: *"Behold the Lamb of God, which taketh away the sin of the world"* (John 1:29).

The bronze altar was built of acacia wood, overlaid with bronze. It was about three cubits (1.6 metres) and had four horns, one at each corner. Even the bronze utensils were intricately described, together with their functionality, such as pots to remove ash, shovels, meat forks and firepans. These were mundane items, yet so essential to the whole operation.

Rings were placed on all the furniture for easy removal until again required.

The Covenant between God and the people of Israel was confirmed when Moses sprinkled blood against the altar and then on the people. From earliest times, altars were made from various materials including stone and other available items. From the time Moses spent on Mount Sinai, the design became more specific: *"Make the altar hollow, out of boards. It is to be made just as you were shown on the mountain"* (Exodus 27:8). This form of worship was ongoing between the Lord and Israel as the sacrifices continued in temple worship during the lifetime of Christ.

The Interior

The interior of the tabernacle was divided into two departments by a veil. The first room was called the 'Holy Place', and the second the 'Holiest of All'.

The Holy Place
The Holy Place contained three articles of furniture:

1. Bread of Presence Table
The Bread of Presence table signified God's presence over His chosen people and was located on the northern side in the Holy Place. The table and the poles which carried the table were made of acacia wood covered with gold. The plates and dishes were also gold.

On the table were placed twelve loaves of bread for the twelve tribes of Israel, representing a perpetual offering to the Lord. The loaf offerings acknowledged the fruit of their labour and that all they enjoyed was by God's blessing. The loaves were renewed weekly then given to Aaron and his sons:

> It belongs to Aaron and his sons, who are to eat it in the sanctuary area because it is a holy part of their perpetual share of the food offerings presented to the Lord.
> *(Leviticus 24:9)*

2. Lampstands

The lampstands were the most ornate objects in the tabernacle; the filigree work was impressive. God reminded the people to take care to construct the lampstands according to the pattern shown to Moses on the mountain. The lamps which stood on the south side of the Holy Place were regularly supplied with pure olive oil and trimmed every morning and evening. They were not to be extinguished at the one time, as a reminder to worshippers that God is the eternal light. This tradition has been continued in many churches of today:

> Make a lampstand of pure gold. Hammer out its base and shaft, and make its flowerlike cups, buds and blossoms of one piece with them. Six branches are to extend from the sides of the lampstand – three on one side and three on the other. Three cups shaped like almond flowers with buds and blossoms... Then make its seven lamps...
> *(Exodus 25:31–37)*

3. Altar of Incense

This second altar, also made with acacia wood and covered with gold, stood on the west side of the Holy Place. The Lord instructed Aaron to burn sweet spices when he lit the lamps every morning and evening. The ingredients of the incense as described by the Lord were gum resin, onycha, and galbanum – pure frankincense, all in equal parts. The fragrance from the smoke symbolised the people's prayers wafting up to heaven.

Other Biblical references to the prayers of God's people rising as sweet-smelling incense are found throughout the Bible. These prayers were generally accompanied by raising hands. The incense altar was also used once a year when Aaron made atonement on its horn for the people. The atonement was made with the blood of the atoning sin offerings:

> Once a year Aaron shall make atonement on its horns. This annual atonement must be made with the blood of the atoning sin offering for the generations to come. It is most holy to the Lord."
> *(Exodus 30:10)*

David, when calling to God to hear him, wrote:

> Let my prayer be set before you as incense. The lifting up of my hands be like the evening sacrifice.
> *(Psalm 141:2)*

Incense burning continued into New Testament times. Zachariah's division was on duty as priest before the Lord, and as he was burning the incense while many people were praying outside, the Angel Gabriel came and told him of the birth of John:

> When the time for burning of incense came, all the assembled worshipers were praying outside.
> *(Luke 1:10)*

Holy of Holies

The Holy of Holies was separated from the Holy Place by a thick curtain, and it contained two most holy articles – The Ark of the Covenant and the Mercy Seat.

1. The Ark of the Covenant

Exodus 19–25 tells us that the Ark of the Covenant (the Ark) was revealed to Moses on Mount Sinai, and it was to be the first and most sacred piece of tabernacle furniture. Through the Ark, God would meet with Moses to discuss His sovereign plan. After the high priesthood was established, only the High Priest Aaron could enter the Holy of Holies annually with blood to make atonement for himself and his people.

As with the other furnishings, the Ark was made of acacia wood covered with gold and fitted with rings, through which rods were placed for transportation. The main function of the Ark was to hold sacred objects, the most important being the two stones on which Moses wrote the Ten Commandments.

The other two objects were a pot of manna and later Aaron's staff which blossomed confirming God's appointment of Aaron as high priest (Numbers 17:1–12).

2. The Mercy Seat

The Ark had a lid made of solid gold called the Mercy Seat. On the lid were two golden cherubim with outstretched wings and downcast eyes. It was thought that God was enthroned between the wings, thus making the Ark a symbol of God's presence. In Hezekiah's prayer, he confirmed this belief that the Ark was the throne or footstool to the throne of God's presence on earth:

> Hezekiah prayed to the Lord: 'Lord, the God of Israel, enthroned between the cherubim, you alone are God over all kingdoms of the earth.'
> *(2 Kings 19:15)*

The Holy of Holies was so sacred that only the high priest was permitted to enter this sanctuary, and then just once a year, during the Day of Atonement in October. On that occasion he would sprinkle the blood of the sacrifice on the Mercy Seat, first for his own sins and then for the sins of the people. Above the entire Ark dwelt the glory, the cloud of God – 'Shekinah glory'.

The writer of the book of Hebrews, in his reverence of temple imagery, recalled the temple treasures. He provided an elaborate description of one sacred object – the Ark of the Covenant:

> The first covenant had regulations for worship and also an earthly sanctuary. A tabernacle was set up. In its first room were the lampstand and the table with its consecrated bread; this was called the Holy Place. Behind the second curtain was a room called the Most Holy Place, which had the golden altar of incense and the gold-covered ark of the covenant. This ark contained the gold jar of manna, Aaron's staff that had budded, and the stone tablets of the covenant. Above the ark were the cherubim of the Glory, overshadowing the atonement cover. But we cannot discuss these things in detail now.
>
> *(Hebrews 9:1–5)*

Hebrews 9:5 concludes with an assumption that there was much more to learn from the Ark, but the writer indicated that further discussion was to be for another time. He then expanded on this concept in Hebrews 9:8:

> The Holy Spirit was showing by this, that the way into the Most Holy Place had not yet been disclosed.

Special Skills

God did not allow just anyone to work on His sacred abode, the tabernacle; He chose people whom He knew were skilled in the requirements of each task. One of the earliest instances of the Spirit of God coming upon people and equipping them for a particular task is referenced in Exodus 31:2–6:

> I have chosen Bezalel son of Uri ... I have filled him with the Spirit of God, with wisdom, with understanding, with knowledge and with all kinds of skills – to make artistic designs for work in gold, silver and bronze, to cut and set stones, to work in wood, and to engage in all kinds of crafts. Moreover, I have appointed Oholiab son of Ahisamak, of the tribe of Dan, to help him. Also, I have given ability to all the skilled workers to make everything I have commanded you.

Furthermore, God gave the ability to other skilled workers who remained unnamed:

> For the entrance to the courtyard, provide a curtain twenty cubits long, of blue, purple and scarlet yarn and finely twisted linen – the work of an embroiderer.
> *(Exodus 27:16)*

These beautiful verses have reached into the hearts of many creative persons throughout history who have had the privilege to serve God in His houses of worship. Although these include great preachers and teachers, there are many more people whose gifts and abilities continue to glorify God today. They include the creators of great cathedrals, schools, works of art and literature, and other beautiful icons.

The Hebrews from the tabernacle times onwards have treasured their literature and other holy relics of their faith. All the articles, together with the materials that went into the building of the tabernacle, created a riot of colour, texture, and design. Each of these elements embraced the whole of their senses – sight, touch, and emotions, making it a joy to behold.

This was where God came down to dwell among His people, and here we have similarities to much of what was revealed to us in God's throne room. All these dyes and materials which were identified in Exodus were available in Egypt during the time of Moses, as Egypt had used the techniques of weaving for up to fifteen centuries prior to this period.

Dedication of the Tabernacle

The tabernacle and all equipment were dedicated by Moses on the first day of the first month in the second year. Exodus 40 tells us that the final activities were setting up the courtyard around the tabernacle, which housed the altar and putting up the curtain at the entrance of the courtyard *"... so Moses finished the work!"*

Anointing Oil

Prior to the dedication of the tabernacle, its furnishings, along with Aaron and his sons, were anointed with oil. The anointing oil and the incense were sacred, and the people were forbidden to make them for their own use. God said:

> Anoint Aaron and his sons and consecrate them so they
> may serve me as priests.
> *(Exodus 30:30)*

Glory of the Lord

The Glory of the Lord's presence in the form of a cloud filled the tabernacle to such an extent that Moses could not enter it. The cloud continued to hover over the tabernacle during the day with the addition of fire which lit the cloud throughout the night. During the wilderness wandering, the cloud also indicated when the Israelites were to move and when to remain in a camp.

The Ark of the Covenant led the people as they marched forward, which was a time of great rejoicing and praise.

Remarkably, it was just a short time earlier that these unimportant, suppressed, unnamed slaves were kept alive only to construct great buildings and perform other menial tasks for Egyptian dignitaries.

Writings on tablets from El-Amarna from a Canaanite king to the Egyptian pharaoh mentioned the problem of attacks from roving bands of foreigners called the Habiru. The name Habiru possibly represented any homeless or displaced persons, and by this time the descendants of Abraham fell into that category. The Bible tells us that the Pharaoh at the time was becoming concerned that the Hebrews may be a threat to Egypt.

As individuals, they were considered nobodies. However, with slavery behind them, they had become a nation, where each person was unique, and honoured by God and each other. The Hebrew nation had become God's chosen ones, with God himself as the cornerstone of their whole existence, with the decalogue representing the value that God had for all His creation.

Conclusion

It will be revealed that instead of remaining true to their promise to love and worship their Creator God, sadly the Israelites were quick to give their allegiance to the gods of the surrounding nations, eventually to their own destruction. However, even amidst troublesome times, there will always be righteous people who remain true to the Lord and His ways, as Acts 14:17 confirms:

> In the past, he let all nations go their own way, yet he has not left himself without testimony.

20. ISRAEL'S RELIGIOUS LEADERS

Priests and Levites

When the Hebrews were transformed into a holy nation, the Lord gave them the responsibility of representing God and His laws to all nations. God set up a theocracy, a system of government in which priests rule in the name of God, based upon a God-given covenant and rules for living. From the time of Moses to David, the Lord selected a hierarchy of leaders to be in charge of all acts of public worship, and administrative and legal activities, which verified every minute detail of the Israelites' daily activities as under God's control.

As recorded in Genesis, sacrifices were an ancient practice and continued as part of religious observances throughout the Old Testament. Prior to the construction of the tabernacle and the appointment of the priesthood, the patriarchs offered sacrifices. The concept of a priesthood was not entirely new. From the beginning of time when nations were established, the people felt compelled to worship gods and goddesses by setting aside a priestly caste to lead the services and festivals. Priestly families were chosen to fulfil the various tasks required to ensure their gods were worshipped in a suitable manner, and that the buildings were maintained.

The nations' rulers generally controlled the religious life of their people, and the priestly caste were treated with exceptional respect and honour, even the authentic pattern of the tabernacle resembled the temples of these nations. The greatest difference between Israel's patterns of worship and other nations, was that everything was connected with structure and worship based on a theocracy, with the tribe of Levi being chosen to provide priests, singers and other personnel to act as artisans and other craftsmen.

Levites

God's choice of the Levites was a result of their loyalty to God when the Israelites rebelled after the corrupt incident of the golden calf. Following the instructions from God, Moses stood at the entrance of the camp where the Levites rallied with him and destroyed many of the evildoers. Moses then said to the Levites:

> You have been set apart to the Lord today, for you were against your own sons and brothers, and he has blessed you this day.
> *(Exodus 32:29)*

This display of loyalty appeared to account for the special responsibilities given to the tribe of Levi as ministers in the tabernacle. The Levites' first role was to replace, in their religious status, all the firstborn of Israel who were consecrated to God on the night of the Passover. The Lord said to Moses:

> Consecrate to me every firstborn male. The first offspring of every womb among the Israelites belongs to me, whether human or animal.
> *(Exodus 13:2)*

Moses then reiterated to the people:

> You are to give over to the LORD the first offspring of every womb. All the firstborn males of your livestock belong to the Lord.
> *(Exodus 13:12)*

The members of these families were trained from birth for their God-given tasks. The eligible age for taking care of God's tent ranged from thirty to fifty years, although the age limits could vary.

Office of the Priesthood

The appointment of Aaron as High Priest, a fourth generation of Levi, marked the commencement of a priestly dynasty. At this time, the position was normally hereditary for life. Despite many upheavals and changes to the office of priesthood, the position continued for more than a thousand years, until the Romans put an end to it when the temple was destroyed in 70 AD.

Aaron's office of High Priest played a dominant role in the observance of the rituals of the tabernacle. Numbers Chapter 18 makes it clear that only Aaron and his sons could serve as priests. The Lord said to Aaron:

> You, your sons and your family are to bear the responsibility for offenses connected with the sanctuary, and you and your sons alone are to bear the responsibility for offenses connected with the priesthood.
> Only you and your sons may serve as priests in connection with everything at the altar and inside the curtain. I am giving you the service of the priesthood as a gift.
> *(Numbers 18:1, 7)*

Aaron and his sons were thus consecrated to lead the people in worship, being placed in charge of the shrines and sanctuaries, together with officiating at the sacrifices and the offering of incense on behalf of the Israelites.

Other duties of the priestly caste included blessing the people, teaching the laws of God, including general ethical instructions, and ritual and legal cases.

> If cases come before your courts that are too difficult for you to judge… go to the Levitical priests and to the judge who is in office at that time. Inquire of them and they will give you the verdict.
> *(Deuteronomy 17:8–9)*

Conditions Relevant to the Priestly Caste

Holiness of life was considered the first attribute of the priestly caste. Josephus (1987) noted:

As for the priests, he (Moses) prescribed to them among other things, a double degree of purity, that they be unblemished in all respects. He also enjoined them, not only to observe purity in their sacred ministrations, but also in their daily conversation, that it might be unblameable.

An editor for Josephus, in the section *The Antiquities of the Jews*, (Book 3, Chapter 7, page 83) later noted that there were two further qualifications required for the constitution of the first high priest. The first qualification was that a high priest should have an excellent character for virtuous and good actions. The second was that he should have the commendation of the people.

These qualifications which were the words of God himself, are the same qualifications which the Christian religion requires when choosing bishops, priests, and deacons, as written in the *Apostolic Constitutions: Book Two (Apostolic Constitutions: Book II* (1886/2021). These are two of the many links between Jewish culture and worship, and the formation of the guidelines of worship and behaviour of Christians.

The conditions given to the priests in the Old Testament were reinforced in the early church:

> Here is a trustworthy saying: Whoever aspires to be an overseer desires a noble task. Now the overseer is to be above reproach, faithful to his wife, temperate, self-controlled, respectable, hospitable, able to teach.
> *(1 Timothy 3:1–2)*

These requirements are indications that the eternal God's expectations of Christian leaders, like the Jewish leaders, have not changed throughout the centuries. Holiness of life and respect of God's ritual and worship, are not only for Church leaders but for all who seek the Lord.

Office of the High Priest

Alfred Edersheim (1874/1994) noted that although Aaron's sons were vital in the smooth running of the sacrificial offerings, the characteristics of the priesthood and it's functions were centred in the person of the high priest, namely Aaron. The original meaning of the Hebrew term for priest – *cohen/kohen*, as explained by Edersheim, means "one who stands up for another and mediates his cause". Edersheim also expanded this concept of mediation when he recorded:

> The fundamental ideas which underlay all activities and connecting them into a harmonious whole, were 'reconciliation' and 'mediation': the one expressed by typically atoning sacrifices, the other by a typically intervening priesthood.

These two concepts resulted in a harmonious whole, connecting God with His people. The high priest had three further requirements to observe which are not generally in practice today:

- He could not mourn the dead

- He had to avoid being near any dead body, which could cause defilement
- He could only marry a virgin.

The Consecration

Everything about the consecration ceremony pointed to the eternal God and His holiness:

- He would abide with His people but there could be no familiarity
- He alone outlined the way He was to be approached
- Sin disqualified anyone, great or small, from entering His presence
- The priests and everything else had to be set apart for God's service.

Aaron and his sons therefore needed to be cleansed, robed, and their sins atoned by sacrifice before they could take office.

Ceremony of Ordination

The consecration of a Levite family member to the Israelite priesthood was one of the most spectacular ceremonies in the Old Testament. They would have been chosen for this office at an early age, and ordination was a sacred procedure. All of Israel watched the preliminaries of the consecration of the priests and Levites. They were bathed with water, clothed, and anointed with oil (Exodus 29:4, 7). Anointing incense consisted of liquid myrrh, fragrant cinnamon and calamus, cassia, and a hint of olive oil (Exodus 30:22–24). As with every other creation, the manufacture of this incense was entrusted to an experienced perfumer.

Lastly, the priests and Levites were identified with a sacrifice (Exodus 29:15-20), which was performed by laying their hands on the dying lamb. The blood of the lamb was then placed on it's right ear, right thumb, and right big toe. The blood on the hand and toe indicated that the whole person was dedicated to the Lord's service and his willingness to hear and carry out God's instructions.

Garments of the Priests (Cahahaeae)

The imagery of garments and clothing have great significance in the Bible. The robes of the priests and Levites contained much symbolism and imagery, designed to direct the worshippers upward to the Lord and his Holiness. Moses described in detail the clothing of the tabernacle personnel. He was as meticulous in this as he was with the holy furniture. For an appointment into these holy offices, God instructed Moses to make garments for the priests that were both practical and beautiful, as precious as any garment created for any royal personage:

> Have Aaron your brother brought to you from among the Israelites, along with his sons Nadab and Abihu, Eleazar and Ithamar, so they may serve me as priests. Make sacred garments for your brother Aaron to give him dignity and honour. Tell all the skilled workers to whom I have given wisdom in such matters that they are to make garments for Aaron, for his consecration, so he

may serve me as priest. These are the garments they are to make: a breastpiece, an ephod, a robe, a woven tunic, a turban and a sash. They are to make these sacred garments for your brother Aaron and his sons, so that they may serve me as priests. Have them use gold, and blue and purple and scarlet yarn, and fine linen.
(Exodus 28:1–5)

Three Categories of Priestly Garments

Every part of the priestly and Levitical robes represented spiritual symbolism. All who came into the Lord's presence had to be dressed for the occasion as every part of the attire was chosen as a reminder of God's holiness and care for His people. The ordinary priests wore four white linen garments all year round. They consisted of breeches which extended to the knees and tied at the top with a cord. The garments were identical to the white garments worn by the high priest on the Day of Atonement.

Tunic

On top of the garments used by Aaron and his sons in ministering in the sanctuary, was a tunic of fine linen with embroidered work in the royal yarn colours of blue, purple, and scarlet. The tunic was designed to extend from the neck down to the feet just above the heels and hang close to the body. A sash and a cap, which many believe was wound in a conical shape, were also included.

Garments of the High Priest

The superiority of Aaron's attire over the rest of the priesthood was indicated by differences in quality and colour to those of the other priests. Aaron's role as High Priest was so important that the Lord chose the finest linen and imperial colours to ensure that the people respected their religious leaders. This regalia, which was worn all year round, consisted of eight garments called the 'golden garments'. These garments consisted of robe, ephod, tunic, breeches, an embroidered coat, breastplate, turban, and sash, which are all described in great detail in Exodus Chapters 28 and 39.

Robe of the Ephod

The robe of the ephod was a violet seamless outer garment, with an opening at the neck and bound so it would remain intact. It was always worn under the ephod, being longer than the ephod and extended from the shoulder to below the knees. Along the hem were blue, purple, and scarlet pomegranates and golden bells (panonim) which tinkled as the priest served in the tabernacle.

> The sound of the bells will be heard when he enters the
> Holy Place before the Lord and when he comes out,
> so he will not die.
> *(Exodus 28:35–36)*

A commentator from *The Works of Josephus* (1987) proposed an explanation of the embellishment on the robe of the ephod:

By shaking his garment at the time of his offering incense in the temple, on the great day of expiation, or at other proper periods of his sacred ministrations there, his people might notice and might as one offer those common prayers jointly with the priest himself to the Almighty.

The son Sirach, an apocryphal writer, showed another further insight, when he said of Aaron, the first high priest:

> God encompassed Aaron with pomegranates and with many bells round about, that as he went there might be a sound, and a noise made that might be heard in the temple, for a memorial to the children of his people (Sirach 14:9).

Ephod

One of the most important garments of the high priest was the ephod. This was made of gold, blue, purple, and scarlet yarn of fine linen. It was worn on the top of his other garments with a front like an apron. A waistband was used just under the heart to keep everything together. Attached to the waistband were two shoulder straps, shaped like braces, which came up from the back and continued over the shoulders. Fastened on each shoulder by a golden clasp were two onyx stones with the names of the six tribes on each, called 'stones of remembrance'.

Breastplate of Judgement

When the high priest entered the Holy Place, he wore the breastplate attached to the shoulders with two golden chains directly under two onyx stones. These chains extended from the settings of two golden rings to fasten the breastplate to the ephod, and which was made of the same royal colours of the ephod – gold, blue, purple and scarlet. Like the onyx stones, the breastplate was set with four rows of three small stones placed in gold. Each of these stones represented one of the twelve tribes of Israel. The Bible reminds us that the purpose of these stones was to be *"a memorial before the Lord continually"* (Exodus 28:29).

Urim and Thummim

In Exodus 28:30, God explains the use of the Urim and Thummim:

> Put the Urim and the Thummim in the breastplate, so that they may be over Aaron's heart whenever he enters the presence of the Lord.

The Urim and Thummim were used to cast lots for questions needing a 'yes' or 'no' answer from God.

Chiam Richman (1997) wrote:

> According to most authoritative opinions, the expression 'Urim and Thummim' actually refers not to the breastplate itself, but the mystical divine name of God, which was

written on a piece of parchment and inserted into a flap of the garment.

Turban

> Then he placed the turban on Aaron's head and set the gold plate, the sacred emblem, on the front of it, as the Lord commanded Moses.
> *(Leviticus 8:9)*

The words engraved upon the front of the golden nameplate were 'Holiness unto the Lord'.

Sash

Two sashes were used by the high priest for different occasions. One was created with finely twined linen, embroidered with blue, purple, and scarlet needlework, and designed to be used throughout the year. The other was created with white linen, for use on the Day of Atonement. The prophet Ezekiel recognised these sacred garments:

> When they (the priests) go out into the outer court where the people are, they are to take off the clothes they have been ministering in and are to leave them in the sacred rooms, and put on other clothes, so that the people are not consecrated through contact with their garments.
> *(Ezekiel 44:17–19)*

Chiam Richman (1997) posed the question:

> Why does the Bible attach so much significance to the garments? Because they possess a certain holiness, powerful enough to sanctify all those who merely come in contact with them.

Day of Atonement – Yom Kippur

Every year on the Day of Atonement, the High Priest alone was allowed to carry out the sacred tasks to be performed on that day. He was also permitted to enter the Holy of Holies to make atonement for himself, his priests, and all the other Israelites. After the High Priest bathed himself with water, he was clothed in white garments made of six-ply linen representing holiness for the Day of Atonement. The garments were: linen undergarments – worn next to the body, two linen tunics – one for morning, one for evening, a white sash, and a white linen turban (mitre). When he had finished with these clothes, he never wore them again.

Assisting Levites

When Aaron and his sons were ordained as priests, all other Levites became assistants. As recorded in Numbers 3:6–13, the Lord said to Moses:

> Bring the tribe of Levi and present them to Aaron the priest to assist him. They are to perform duties for him and for the whole community at the tent of meeting by

doing the work of the tabernacle. They are to take care of all the furnishings of the tent of meeting, fulfilling the obligations of the Israelites by doing the work of the tabernacle... The Levites are mine ... I am the Lord.

The Levites were appointed as guards around the tabernacle. They camped and served as protective buffers to the other tribes who were threatened with God's wrath if they unwittingly came in contact with the Holy Tabernacle and its furnishing. Eleazar was Chief of the Levites, and Ithamar was responsible for the care of the tabernacle. The work was divided into three families of Levites, each given certain duties to perform (Numbers 3:30–35).

Sons of Kohath – supervised by Eleazor

The Kohathites were camped on the south side of the tabernacle. They cared the furniture of the tabernacle.

Sons of Merari – supervised by Ithamar

The Merarites were camped on the northern side of the tabernacle and had the task of hauling and constructing the frame of the tabernacle and its outer court.

Sons of Gershon – supervised by Ithamar

The Gershonites were camped on the west side of the tabernacle, and were responsible for the care of the tabernacle, tent, and its coverings.

Remuneration of the Temple Staff

The priests and Levites who were responsible for the care of the Lord's tabernacle were respected and paid abundantly for their work. They were supported by the Israelite's tithes and offerings, one tenth of all harvests and livestock given to God, as well as parts of the meat or grain sacrifices (Numbers 31:25–31).

The sons of Levi shared in tribal rejoicing and the abundance of the chief festivals, especially the Feast of Weeks, as well as sharing the spoils of battle. The spoils were equally divided between the soldiers and the rest of the people. The soldiers were then required to give a tribute, a half-share of what they received, to the high priest Eleazar as the Lord's part.

Benediction of the Tabernacle

With so much colour and pageantry, the dedication of the tabernacle would have been a grand affair. It provided opportunities for the Israelites to witness the artifacts made by the skilled artisans in the gifts they had contributed from the items they had brought out of Egypt.

When the sacrifices were completed, the prayers of gratitude flowed directly to heaven. The Lord then gave Moses a prayer of blessing for the first High Priest to be the anointed:

> Tell Aaron and his sons, 'This is how you are to bless the Israelites. Say to them: The LORD bless you and keep you; the LORD make his face shine on you and be gracious to you; the LORD turn his face toward you and give you peace.'
> *(Numbers 6:23–26)*

This priestly blessing has resounded throughout the world. Firstly, as part of Jewish worship, and then adopted by the Christian church as a final blessing of many services. It has a continuing history in large cathedrals, in other gatherings of Christian worship, in private meetings, and in homes of the faithful. It has reached into the hearts of many, great and small.

The Silver Scrolls

Pastor Gary Kent (2022), speaker for The Incredible Journey ministry in Australia and New Zealand, which is aired on television on Sunday mornings , recounted the find of two old, silver scrolls at Ketef Hinnom in Jerusalem by Archaeologist Gabi Barkay. The dig consisted of searching a number of caves which had been used as tombs. Many treasures were found, among which were two small silver scrolls called amulets, which had holes through their centres so the amulets could be worn around the necks of the Israelites.

These fragile scrolls were finally sent to the Israeli Museum in Jerusalem where they were carefully unrolled. The inscription on the scrolls shocked the people involved as the message in the scrolls was the Priestly Benediction which Moses had received from the Lord for Aaron to bless the people.

The silver scrolls were four hundred years older than the Dead Sea Scrolls, and when translated they were found to be in accordance with many English translations of the Bible. One such example is:

> The Lord bless you and keep you
> The Lord make his face shine on you
> and be gracious to you
> The Lord turn his face toward you
> and give you peace.
> *(Numbers 6:23–26)*

The age of these silver scrolls appears to authenticate the Pentateuch.

When Moses of the tribe of Levi blessed the Israelites from his deathbed, he particularly noted their spirituality, responsibility, and loyalty. He stated about Levi:

> Your Thummim and Urim belong to your faithful servant… but he watched over your word and guarded your covenant. He teaches your precepts to Jacob and your law to Israel.
> He offers incense before you and whole burnt offerings on your altar. Bless all his skills, Lord, and be pleased with the work of his hands…
> *(Deuteronomy 33:8–11)*

Music Used in Tabernacle Worship

As seen above, when the Hebrews were travelling through the wilderness for forty years, no group of Levites were put in charge of the worship music of the tabernacle. There were three sources of music; the first being the tingling of the golden bells which were woven with pomegranates on the hem of the robe:

> The golden bells and the pomegranates are to alternate around the hem. Aaron must wear it when he ministers. The sound of the bells will be heard when he enters the Holy Place before the Lord and when he comes out, so that he will not die.
> *(Exodus 28:34–35)*

Two other instruments used during the offering and sacrifices were the shofar and the silver trumpets.

The Shofar – Ram's Horn

The shofar horns of animals were hollowed out and often elaborately carved. On these instruments, flourishes (signals) were played on occasions. All tube instruments gave only a series of notes, called harmonics or overtones, which were produced by gradually increasing the pressure of air being blown through the embouchure (how the mouth is applied to the mouthpiece of the instrument). The actual sound of the shofar was a mournful, though piercing, sound.

There were three types of shofar tones set down in the *Mishna*, the oldest known codification of Jewish oral laws (as cited in Glaser & Glaser, 1987):

The manner of sounding is three of three each. The length of the sustained note is the same as quavering notes. The length of a quavering note is equal to that of three wailing notes. If one sounded the first sustained note and then prolonged the second note for as long as two, it counts only as one. If one had already recited the benediction, then happened to obtain a shofar, he should sound three times a sustained note, a quavering note, and a sustained note. (Jerusalem Talmud Rosh Hashanah 4:9)

The Silver Trumpets (Kjatsotsrah – Hazozra)

The Lord gave Moses specific instructions on how to fashion the silver trumpets, as well as ordaining when and how it was to be blown.

Assembling, Marching, and Battle

For the Israelites, two trumpets blasted; for the heads of clans, one trumpet sounded. The blast (flourish) was the signal for moving the camp. At the first trumpet blast, the tribes on the east side set out; at the sound of the second blast, the camps on the south side followed. When they went into battle in their own land, a blast on the trumpets was sounded, at which time they were remembered by the Lord.

Memorial, New Moon Festivals, and Offerings

The trumpet blasts acted as a memorial for the Israelites before their God. The shofar, together with the tishri (silver trumpet), signalled the beginning of each month. These trumpets also sounded over their burnt offering and the fellowship offers:

> They will be a memorial for you before your God.
> *(Numbers 10:10)*

Year of Jubilee (Shemittah – Chabad)

The blast of the shophar announced the Year of Jubilee. As noted above, temple music was limited to trumpet blowing, either for assembly or as the commencement ritual acts. Later, David did much to prepare the musicians, both vocal and instrumental for Solomon's Temple, where it would become as a pageantry of the worship, a glorious scene to behold.

Summary of the Building of the Tabernacle

The tabernacle portrayed an edifice of architectural and artistic delight. It embraced all the elements of good design – functionality, workability for the job in hand, and materials which were adaptable whether stationary or on the move. It survived through the dusty desert for forty years, and continued to be the centre of worship until the first permanent temple was constructed.

The riot of colour is a reminder to every believer of the vivid beauty and colour which were displayed in God's heavenly abode. This beauty was continued in His tabernacle on earth. The sole purpose of the tabernacle was that through the daily ritual of many sacrifices and prayer, the Israelites might be constantly reminded of their need to worship the Lord in every part of their lives.

The priestly attire was perfect for its function, with each part designed to represent some aspect of God's holiness and care for His people – the twelve tribes of Israel were forever before Him. These robes survived tenaciously until the times of Christ, and later similar apparel was adopted by many churches for priests and lay-people who led Christian worship through the centuries.

Conclusion

The Lord himself chose the priests who were to serve Him in His Holy Place, together with the requirements of a holy life that was chosen for all priests, Levites, and Israelites, with dire consequences if they sinned.

To assist them in their quest for Holiness, the significance of much of the apparel was designed as a constant reminder of God and of His Love for all.

21. RITUAL PATTERNS OF WORSHIP

An understanding of the ritual patterns of the Bible lead to a greater understanding of the holiness of God, and our response to this holiness. Ritual patterns are evident in all formal worship throughout the world, even if the adherents do not recognise any organised structure. We humans like to have ordered patterns in our lives as they give a sense of security and belonging to our existence.

Communal oral repetition was used continually in the lives of the Israelites in their homes and in corporate worship in the tabernacle. For instance, the slaying of beasts began with Abel and was continued by the believers and the unbelievers throughout history. This ritualistic act was a perpetual reminder to the Israelites that through death, life is obtained. During the patriarchal period, a beast was slain for a family, and with the construction of the tabernacle, the blood was shed for the whole congregation.

Ritual was not only passive, being given instructions on how to act, but was also an active response to what was said. It began within the home, as parents trained their children to become trustworthy adults. The process was by means of oral repetition and continually proving what was right. Even as early as the Pentateuch, the Lord, on at least three such occasions, gave instructions to parents to continually remind their children by using such teaching aids as phylacteries (or in Hebrew, tefillin), which were placed on their left arm and forehead:

> "On that day tell your son, 'I do this because of what the Lord did for me when I came out of Egypt. This observance will be for you like a sign on your hand and a reminder on your forehead that this law of the Lord is to be on your lips...'"
> *(Exodus 13:8–9)*

The phylacteries consisted of two small leather cases bound by leather straps to the forehead and left forearm. They were worn by adult males at daily morning prayers, at home or in the synagogue, except on the Sabbath and high festivals. These were worn in a prescribed manner so as to represent the letters 'shin', 'daleth' and 'yodh', and when combined, formed the divine name *Shaddai*, meaning 'the Almighty' (Eerdmans, 1986). Texts from the Torah were inscribed on parchment and placed in each phylactery. Verses in Deuteronomy confirm the importance of using these as reminders of their faith in the Lord and His word:

> Impress them upon your children... Tie them as symbols on your hands and bind them on your foreheads. Write them upon the door frames of your houses and on your gates.
> *(Deuteronomy 6:7–9)*

In the New Testament, Jesus warned His followers of the pharisees and teachers who were misusing God's reminders of Himself for their own religious enhancement. Sometimes, people today may observe others using God-given ritualistic objects and sacred icons, and erroneously judge the inanimate things, rather than act as Christ did by righteously judging those who wrongfully use the icons to enhance themselves.

The Calendar

From earliest times, the Hebrews were given instructions on holy days and festivals as part of their religion and way of life. Awareness of God's presence and holiness was central to all their activities. Like the nations around them, the Hebrew festivals celebrated the seasons of the year, such as seedtime and harvest, which were held in spring, early summer, and autumn. The occasions were celebrated in gratitude for God's yearly blessings.

Graeme A. Brady (1983) added another dimension when he proposed:

> In the Hebrew religion, these nature festivals were overshadowed by the annual commemoration of an historical event – the deliverance by God of a slave people from Egypt.

Furthermore, Glaser and Glaser (1987) asserted:

> The Hebrews sensed a holy obligation to live obediently before the Lord of time. If God had expressly designed a calendar, it was their duty to observe it properly. To the pious, it was no small thing if a new moon was mistaken,

and the appointed times of the Lord were observed on the wrong days. The Lord of the calendar was to be obeyed with heart-felt precision.

Throughout Biblical history, after each time of repentance and reformation, the Jews sought the Scriptures to recall what was required from the Lord, to permit them to return to God and His ways.

Appointed Times of the Lord

Leviticus 23 describes nine appointed times of the Lord, together with the celebration of the new moon:

> The Lord said to Moses: 'Speak to the Israelites and say to them: 'These are my appointed feasts, the feasts of the Lord, which you are to proclaim as sacred assemblies.'
> *(Leviticus 23:1–2)*

After God had announced the order of the Hebrew calendar, the beginning of every month and every other festival was announced by the priests with a blast of trumpets:

> The Lord said to Moses: "At your times of rejoicing – your appointed festivals and New Moon feasts – you are to sound the trumpets over your burnt offerings and fellowship offerings, and they will be a memorial for you before your God. I am the Lord your God."
> *(Numbers 10:1, 10)*

Sabbath – One Day of Rest in Seven

The pattern of the Sabbath was foreordained in God's six days of creation followed by a day of rest on the seventh. It was not a feast, but a holy assembly, a time set apart after six days of work for religious activities and sacrifices. This was Israel's most distinctive holy day. Frey (2011) explains that the Sabbath was not only given to the Israelites, but like other gifts of God, the cessation of work for the Israelites was meant for the whole world and signified the Creator's presence and care for His world.

The Sabbath encapsulated God's presence in the world, regardless of the world's nature and condition. During this time, the Israelites were to remember all that God had done for them, in particular their rescue from slavery in Egypt.

New Moon

With no written calendar available, the day of the new moon was announced by priests blowing silver trumpets signalling the beginning of each month. On this day, the priests offered special sacrifices and a grain offering which together produced a pleasing aroma to the Lord:

> With each bull there is to be a drink offering of half a hin of wine; with the ram, a third of a hin; and with each lamb, a quarter of a hin. This is the monthly burnt offering to be made at each new moon during the year.
> *(Numbers 28:14)*

Note: A hin is a Hebrew unit of liquid capacity equal to approximately five litres.

The precise determination of the new moon was important to the Israelites – not knowing the exact time of the new moon could disrupt their entire calendar.

Sabbatical Year

Just as every seventh day was a day of rest for the people, God also provided times of rest for the land every seven years when they entered Canaan. The significance of this was to remind the Israelites that the land was not their own, it was holy and belonged to the Lord. Additionally, every seventh year all Israelite slaves were set free.

Jubilee Year

The Jubilee Year reminded the Israelites that the land belonged to the Lord. This also prevented the wealthy from accumulating additional property. It was also a year of restoration – if anyone had fallen on bad times, they were granted freedom, and their properties were restored. Whatever had grown on the land during these times of rest, belonged to everyone – their own countrymen and foreigners.

Renowned economist Michael Hudson (2018) reveals the relevance of ancient civilisation economies for today's society in his book ... *And Forgive Them Their Debts*. Hudson states:

The idea of annulling debts nowadays seems so unthinkable that most economists and many theologians doubt whether the Jubilee Year could have been applied in practice, indeed on a regular basis. A widespread impression is that the Mosaic debt jubilee was a utopian idea. However, Assyriologists have traced it to a long tradition of the Near Eastern reclamations. Instead of causing economic crises, these debt jubilees preserved stability in nearly all new Eastern societies. Economic polarisation, bondage and collapse occurred when such clean slates stopped many in modern terms from being proclaimed 'bankrupt'.

Regular Fast Days
The Israelites fasted and prayed as a genuine sign of repentance.

Offerings of the Tabernacle
There were four main offerings which became the ritual of the tabernacle, as described in Leviticus Chapters 1–5:
- burnt offering – a token of dedication in which the whole animal was burnt
- peace offering – for a restoration of the fellowship between the participant and God
- meal offering – often an accompaniment to the burnt and peace offerings
- sin offering – created to obtain forgiveness.

Burnt Offering

Burnt offerings were the first sacrifices, as they were used every morning and evening, as well as for every Sabbath, the first day of the month, and at special feasts (Numbers 10:10). This voluntary offering was celebrated daily as a constant reminder of the people's need to be cleansed from sin.

Animals used for the burnt offering had to be perfect, and the whole animal except the skin was sacrificed. The worshippers placed their hands on the animals to show that it was sacrificed on behalf of the person's sins. The blood of the animal was sprinkled on the altar to show that the life of it had been dedicated to God.

Peace Offering

> The Peace Offering was like the burnt offering, except only the fat was burnt, it symbolised the peace and fellowship between the worshipper and God. It was a free will offering, resulting in a sweet aroma to the Lord.
> *(Leviticus 3:1–17)*

Meal Offering

As the meal offering was a voluntary offering of homage and thanksgiving to God, no blood was shed and it was presented at the same time as the burnt and drink offerings (Numbers 28:1–15). Specific instructions were given as to the ingredients, which were the finest flour without yeast mixed with olive oil. Part of the grain offering was burnt on the altar on behalf of the worshipper; the rest was a contribution to the food supply for the priests.

Sin Offering

There were two types of sin offering: the first was for sins committed unknowingly against the Lord, and against another person; the second was for a deliberate sin. This sin ritual brought defilement and needed to be cleaned. The blood of the sacrifice was sprinkled as a sign that the defilement had been removed through the death which had taken place. The presiding priest ate some of the sacrifice, and if he survived, it would be a sign that God had accepted this act of repentance.

Annual Festivals

Seven periods in the Hebrew year were set apart as festivals or feasts, which were based on the sacrificial altar and worship of God. The feasts were divided into two groups:

- Group One: Those which relate to the Passover – The Paschal Sacrifice, the Feast of Unleavened Bread, the Feast of the First Fruits, and the Day of Pentecost (Glazer & Glazer, 1987)
- Group Two: The sacred month – Feast of Trumpets, the Day of Atonement, and the Feast of Tabernacles.

Group One

Feast of Unleavened Bread and the Passover – Time of our Freedom

The Feast of Unleavened Bread together with the Passover was the first Hebrew celebration and occurred on the fourteenth and fifteenth days in the first month of the year Nisan (March/April). This was a joyful festival to celebrate the nation's deliverance from Egypt.

From the beginning and throughout their wilderness wanderings, the Passover was a family affair, with food symbolising different aspects of slavery and the escape from Egypt; but, by the time of the New Testament it had become the main 'Pilgrim Festival'.

The story began when an angel 'passed over' the houses of the Israelites, sparing them from death by the lamb which was slain on their behalf. The Feast of Unleavened Bread which began on the fifteenth day of the month of Nisan was eaten at the Passover and the week following, reminding the people that the women had no time to let the bread rise before their escape. It was also a hygienic measure, for the yeast would have turned mouldy, thus rendering the bread inedible.

The bitter herbs were a reminder of how the Egyptians made the lives of the Hebrews bitter in Egypt. The first and last days being a 'holy convocation' during which sacrifices were offered.

Feast of the First Fruits – Shavuot (Later Pentecost – a Greek word meaning fifty)

The Offering of First Fruits was given to people to be used when they entered the land of Canaan.

> The Lord said to Moses, Speak to the Israelites and say to them: When you enter the Land, I am going to give you and you reap its harvest, bring to the priest a sheaf of the first grain of your harvest.
> *(Leviticus 23:9–11)*

Group Two

The Fall Feasts of Israel

In the seventh month of the Jewish calendar, the sacred month of Tishri (September/October) came the second group of the great festivals. This consisted of the Feast of Trumpets, the Day of Atonement, and the Feast of Tabernacles.

This offering was held in early spring, on the sixteenth day of Nisan. It was the beginning of the grain harvest when the people brought the first sheaf of grain to the priest, who then waved it before the Lord. A burnt offering, a meal offering, and a drink offering were also needed. No grain was harvested until the offering of the first fruits. Like every other offering, it also reminded the people of their sojourn in Egypt, and their possession of a *"land flowing with milk and honey, you sow in your field"* (Exodus 23).

This was also a week of joyous festivities which was marked

by a liberal spirit toward the Levites, strangers, together with orphans and widows and praise to God (Leviticus 23:9–14). The people brought their offerings to God as a reminder that the land they were entering and everything in it produced was God's gift to them.

The Feast of Trumpets (Rosh Hashanah – Repentance)

On the first day of Tishri (after the exile, the New Year Festival), the Feast of Trumpets was the first of three festivals held during this sacred month. It was called *Yom T'ruah*, 'the day of blowing', later the 'Feast of Trumpets'.

The blowing of the Trumpets reminded the Israelites of the commencement of this most solemn month of the year. It was a day of rest and worship together with a sacrificial offering to the Lord, as a pleasing aroma (Numbers 29:6). This joyful day directed the people's attention to the most sacred festival of the year, the Day of Atonement.

The Day of Atonement (Yom Kippur)

Holiness is the theme of this event. The day after the Feast of Trumpets, on the tenth day of Tishri, the Old Testament law required the Israelites to set apart one day in the year for a national fast. It was called the Day of Atonement, following the one-day Feast of Trumpets, and took place on the tenth day of the seventh month. This was not a joyous occasion, but one of fasting, humility, and thoughts on atoning sin in their midst. It was a day when the whole nation of

Israel confessed their sins and asked for God's forgiveness and cleansing.

Every year on this sacred day, the High Priest alone was permitted to carry out all the sacred tasks performed on that day. He was responsible for every aspect of the divine service, which included fifteen separate sacrifices. It was also the one occasion when Aaron could enter the Holy of Holies, where the Ark representing God's presence was housed. This privilege was permitted only after he had bathed himself and dressed in the required manner.

Aaron finally went into the Holy of Holies – the inner most sacred part of the tabernacle, where he took two goats, the first being sacrificed, and the blood being sprinkled for himself, his household and the whole community of Israel onto the atonement cover and in front of it. He then took the second goat, known as the scapegoat, and after laying his hand on its head, sent it off into the desert as a sign that the people's sins were forgiven.

The Feast of Ingathering/Tabernacles (Sukkot)

After the solemnity of the Day of Atonement, the people celebrated the final festivity of the year. It was a seven-day feast, commencing on the fifteenth day of Tishri, to celebrate the end of the fruit harvest, when the olives and grapes were gathered – hence the name 'ingathering'.

It was the most popular and joyful of all the festivals, and the celebrations included camping out in gardens and roof-tops, in tents or huts made from tree branches. This was a reminder to the Israelites of the forty years they had lived in tents in the desert.

When all the ritual was completed, God showed His satisfaction in a visible token of His presence by a cloud which came to rest on the tent, and all around the tabernacle was filled with the light of God's glory.

The tabernacle continued to be used as the focal centre of the nation's worship for three hundred years until it was replaced by Solomon's Temple.

Conclusion

Worship enacted in the tabernacle was a continuation and confirmation of the Covenant entered at Mount Sinai. The covenant was not the Israelites' bargain with God, but their response to what he had done for them.

> The will of God was not only defined primarily in terms of ritualistic acts, but also in terms of behaviour.

22. MOSES THE SONG WRITER AND JOURNALIST-HISTORIAN

Moses displayed many skills which proved useful throughout his leadership of the Israelites and their desert wanderings. He was a writer and recorded everything the Lord said to him. Tradition states that Moses wrote the first five books of the Old Testament, the Pentateuch:

> When Moses went and told the people all the Lord's words and laws, they responded with one voice, 'Everything the Lord has said we will do.' Moses then wrote down everything the Lord had said.
> *(Exodus 24:3–4)*

From that time, Moses kept a detailed account of the Israelites' exodus from Egypt:

> Here are the stages in the journey of the Israelites when they came out of Egypt by divisions under the leadership of Moses and Aaron. At the Lord's command Moses recorded the stages in their journey.
> *(Numbers 33:1–2)*

Moses was also a skilled poet and songwriter, as shown in his first *Ode to Joy* when he led the people in a victory song (Exodus

15). Following this, Moses wrote Psalm 90 which is considered to be the oldest known psalm ever recorded. It begins with glorifying the everlasting creator:

> A prayer of Moses the man of God
> Lord, you have been our dwelling place
> throughout all generations.
> Before the mountains were born
> or you brought forth the whole world
> from everlasting to everlasting, you are God.
> *(Psalm 90:1-2)*

Moses continued with a prayer that people would realise how fleeting human life is, and with this awareness, would seek to live in such a way that the outcome would result in a return of God's mercy. This mercy would ensure that His people would have as much contentment in the future as they had in the past:

> A thousand years in your sight
> are like a day that has just gone by,
> or like the watch in the night.
> Yet you sweep people away in the sleep of death–
> they are like the new grass of the morning:
> In the morning it springs up new,
> but by evening it is dry and withered.
> *(Psalm 90:4–6)*

Finally, Moses asked God to bring prosperity to the Israelites' daily lives:

> May the favour of the Lord our God rest on us;
> establish the work of our hands for us–
> yes, establish the work of our hands.
> *(Psalm 90:17)*

Moses' psalm became one of the famous psalms in the Old Testament. Then, through Isaac Watts (1674–1748) it was developed in thought and ideas, becoming one of Christianity's eternal hymns, being used for many occasions. Watts lived at a time when singing in churches was restricted to a metrical version of the psalms, a product of the reformed tradition. This resulted in a rule that the psalms were to be sung in metre, ensuring nothing would be added or deleted. Watts and other writers freed themselves from these restrictions, embracing a more liberal approach to the psalter. They began paraphrasing hymns using Christian topics and scripture outside the Book of Psalms, bringing Christian hymnody into the twenty-first century .

When poetic license gained momentum, Watts was free to express this sense of time, of man's insignificance before God, but yet defining the close link between God and man (Temple, 1954). Because of his work creating this style, Watts has been named 'The Father of Hymnody'.

O GOD, OUR HELP IN AGES PAST

O God, our help in ages past,
Our hope for years to come,
Our shelter from the stormy blast,
And our eternal home.

A thousand ages in thy sight
Are like an evening gone,
Short as the watch that ends the night
Before the rising sun.

Time, like an ever-rolling stream,
Bears all its sons away;
They fly forgotten as a dream
Dies at the opening day.

O God our help in ages past,
Our hope for years to come,
Be thou our guard while troubles last,
and our eternal home.

This hymn has been named 'The International Anthem', as it is universal in its appeal, and has been sung countless times wherever English hymns have been sung. These occasions include:

- the school hymn for King Edward VI School where Isaac Watts was a student

- the peel of the tower clock at the Southampton Civic Centre, England
- the church service, 14 April 1912, over which Captain Edward John Smith presided on the morning before the RMS *Titanic* sank
- on board HMS *Prince of Wales* in 1941 at a religious service as part of the conference which created the Atlantic Charter.

Given the significance of Moses, it would be appropriate to review this great man who, with courage and tenacity, led his wayward people throughout their migration from Egypt to the promised land. On Mount Sinai, Moses received from God the laws which not only guided Israel through the centuries, but later became the basis for the judicial laws of many Christian countries.

Throughout the journey, Moses had times of hesitation and doubt, which proved he was a flawed human being. One such defining moment was a reaction to the Israelites when they were bemoaning the lack of water. Moses turned to his people and said:

> Listen, you rebels, must we bring you water out of this rock?
> *(Numbers 20:10)*

Then in a fit of anger he disobeyed God and struck the rock twice:

> Then Moses raised his arm and struck the rock twice with his staff. Water gushed out, and the community and their livestock drank.
> *(Numbers 20:11)*

This action cost him dearly as God declared:

> Because you did not trust me enough to honour me as holy in the sight of the Israelites, you will not bring this community into the land I give them.
> *(Numbers 20:12)*

Later, when Moses was one hundred and twenty years old and near death, he implored the Lord to reconsider His decision, but the Lord was adamant and replied (*Reader's Digest Association*, 1994):

> 'That is enough,' the Lord said. 'Do not speak to me anymore about this matter. Go up to the top of Pisgah and look west and north and south and east. Look at the land with your own eyes, since you are not going to cross this Jordan.'
> *(Deuteronomy 3:26–27)*

This was a great blow to Moses, but at this time his work was not complete.

Moses' Final Song

Nearing the close of his forty years of leading his people through the wilderness, the Lord told Moses to warn His people of their future, unfaithful behaviour. The Lord, knowing that after Moses' death the Israelites would break their vows and promises to Him, asked Moses to write down a song, which he would recite to Joshua before the whole assembly. This is a poetic, prophetic song, which recorded blessings and curses similar to the blessings and curses of the Suzerain contract between the Suzerain king and the vasal King as noted in Chapter 18.

The song spoke of Moses' concern for Israel and commences with an exhortation to heed the Lord's Word. The prophetic content is pointing to what would be the result of their faithfulness in contrast to their waywardness.

Overview of Moses' Song

> Listen, you heavens, and I will speak;
> hear, you earth, the words of my mouth.
> Let my teaching fall like rain
> and my words descend like dew,
> like showers on new grass,
> like abundant rain on tender plants.
> I will proclaim the name of the Lord.
> Oh, praise the greatness of our God!
> He is the Rock, his works are perfect,
> And all his ways are just
> A faithful God who does no wrong
> Upright and just is he.
> *(Deuteronomy 32:1–4)*

This was followed by Moses calling the Israelites to recall God's kindness and loving care throughout their wilderness journey. Moses then reminded the Israelites that throughout their walk with God, from the beginning to the end of the wilderness journey, they persistently showed ingratitude for all He had done:

> Remember the days of old;
> consider the generations long past.
> Ask your father and he will tell you,
> Your elders, and they will explain to you.
> When the Most High gave the nations their inheritance,
> when he divided all mankind,
> he set up boundaries for the peoples
> according to the number of the sons of Israel.
> For the Lord's portion is his people,
> Jacob his allotted inheritance.
> *(Deuteronomy 32:7;9)*

Moses then recalled the weary wanderings in the wilderness:

> In a desert land he found him,
> in a barren and howling waste.
> He shielded him and cared for him:
> he guarded him as the apple of his eye,
> like an eagle that stirs up its nest
> and hovers over its young,
> that spreads its wings to catch them
> and carries them aloft.
> The LORD alone led him;
> no foreign god was with him.
> *(Deuteronomy 32:10–12)*

After expressing the Lord's love for the people who are the 'apple of his eye', meaning the pupil on which sight is carried, he continues, using the imagery of the eagle as it swiftly spreads its wings to protect its young.

Throughout the Bible, the eagle symbolises the speed and power of God's deliverance and God's destruction (*NIV Dictionary of Biblical Imagery*, 1998). Earlier, the Lord used the eagle as an exemplar, to stress His deliverance of the Israelites from Egypt: *You, yourselves have seen what I did to Egypt, how I carried you on eagles' wings and brought you to myself* (Exodus 19:4). At this point, the Lord reminds them that, *He alone led him; no foreign god was with him* (Deuteronomy. 32:12).

The song continues the theme of foreign gods, reminding the people how they turned to worshipping the gods of the land which they had not known. Even after their many misdeeds, Moses concludes his song with a promise of salvation to the entire world and its people.

> Rejoice, you nations, with his people,
> for he will avenge the blood of his servants;
> he will take vengeance on his enemies
> and make atonement for his land and people.
> *(Deuteronomy 32:43)*

Throughout the Book of Deuteronomy, Moses constantly implored the Israelites to remain faithful to their God, reminding them that obeying the Lord would lead to life, and disobedience would result in death. When Moses was nearing the end of his life, he prepared the nation for its God-given destiny by appointing seventy leaders as advisers to ensure they continue this faithfulness. Moses also asked the Lord to appoint a successor – Joshua was the perfect choice. Joshua, who had faithfully walked with Moses from the Egyptian flight and was then with Moses on Mount Sinai to the end of the wilderness wanderings, would have been acutely aware of the enormous task ahead. Two further qualifications Joshua possessed were obvious; great leadership abilities, which became evident during his life in Canaan, and a strong faith in the Lord. Moses encouraged Joshua in the presence of all Israel:

> Be strong and courageous, for you must go with this people. The Lord goes before you and will be with you; he will never leave you nor forsake you. Do not be afraid; do not be discouraged.
> *(Deuteronomy 31:6)*

When summing up the many difficulties faced by Israel's journey through the wilderness, together with their hope for the continuance of their faith and survival as a nation, Moses stressed the need to keep true to the laws and statutes of the Lord. He implored the Israelites to diligently pass these laws and statues on to the forthcoming generations:

> Fix these words of mine in your hearts and minds; tie them as symbols on your hands and bind them on your foreheads. Teach them to your children, talking about them when you sit at home and when you walk along the

road, when you lie down and when you get up. Write them
on the doorframes of your houses and on your gates, so
that your days and the days of your children may be many
in the land the Lord swore to give your ancestors, as many
as the days that the heavens are above the earth.
(Deuteronomy 11:18–21)

When Moses finally died, he was buried by the Lord in a hidden grave at Mount Nebo. God kept the location a secret so that the Israelites would not turn the grave into a shrine of worship and sin against the Lord.

William Williams of Pantycelyn (1717–1791), another great man of God, lived nearly two thousand years after Moses. Williams was considered one of Wales' greatest literary figures, as a writer of hymns, poetry, and prose. He embraced the story of the Israelites who suffered as slaves in Egypt before wandering in the wilderness for forty years prior to being allowed to enter the promised land. Williams was aware that his own people were experiencing a similar situation. During this time, countless people including men, women, and children, sometimes as young as six, worked in coal mines. Their whole working life was spent underground, in intolerable circumstances, being no better-off than slaves. It was extremely dangerous work, with significant injuries and great loss of life through mine flooding and collapse, and explosions when the candles ignited coal gas.

Serious diseases, such as Black Lung which was caused by the black coal dust settled in their lungs, caused great suffering. Yet, out of this darkness and chaos arose a deep faith which expressed itself in joyful singing, resulting in the most glorious choral music being heard in the local churches and anywhere people gathered. The Welsh people led the British Isles into a new, joyful Christian experience, which was for all, rich or poor.

Williams wrote many songs in both the Welsh and English languages, of which the most popular was, 'Guide me O Thou great Jehovah'. This piece was written in a poetic setting describing occurrences of the Israelites' wanderings in which the Lord strengthened them and gave them courage to continue until they reached the river Jordan.

GUIDE ME, O THOU GREAT JEHOVAH

Guide me, O thou great Jehovah,
Pilgrim through this barren land;
I am weak, but thou art mighty;
Hold me with thy powerful hand:
Bread of heaven,
Bread of heaven,
Feed me now and evermore.

Open now the crystal fountain,
When the healing stream doth flow;
Let the fiery, cloudy pillar
Lead me all my journey through:
Strong deliverer,
Strong deliverer;
Be Thou still my strength and shield.

When I tread the verge of Jordan,
Bid my anxious fears subside:
Death of death, and hell's destruction,
Land me safe on Canaan's side:
Songs of praises,
Songs of praises,
I will ever give to Thee.

Conclusion

The epitaph and summation of traditional Jewish reverence for Moses and his accomplishments appears at the end of the Pentateuch:

> Since then, no prophet has risen in Israel like Moses, whom the Lord knew face to face, who did all those signs and wonders the Lord sent him to do in Egypt— to Pharaoh and to all his officials and to his whole land. For no one has ever shown the mighty power or performed the awesome deeds that Moses did in the sight of all Israel.
> *(Deuteronomy 34:10–12)*

During Christ's transfiguration, he journeyed with some of his disciples up a high mountain where he was transfigured before them:

> His face shone like the sun, and his clothes became as white as the light. Just then there appeared before them Moses and Elijah, talking with Jesus.
> *(Matthew 17:2–3)*

THE PENTATEUCH
Summary

In this book, I have argued that the beauty and greatness of art and creation predated the existence of humankind, but were with God in eternity, and reflect His qualities. This book has surveyed the first five books of the Bible, highlighting history, theology and timeless principles that can give insight and guidance to modern Christians today.

As an historical record of the Old Testament, the Pentateuch reports the early existence of humankind, from Adam and Eve to Moses. It encapsulates everything which all people need to know about the Creator God and His laws concerning His holiness and worship together with His requirements for human relationships.

Genesis 1:1 commences – *In the beginning God created the heavens and the earth,* and this seems to be essential to understanding our faith in the twenty-first century. Throughout the Old Testament, knowledge of God, the Father who was introduced in this one verse, is expanded and enlarged giving us a broader concept of His character, His greatness and control of the whole universe, including our earth.

Prior to the creation of all life, the earth and its environs were adapted and modified to ensure that Adam and Eve, together with the countless species of living creatures, would ultimately dwell upon the earth in safety.

Humans as the pinnacle of God's creative activity were all implanted with the image of God, which enabled them to rise to unbelievable heights in the worship of the Lord as He ordained, and to be responsible as caretakers of all other living things.

Early in the creative story, the devil is instructed through the snake. The Scriptures gives much information about this creature, his influence and temptations. Even Christ himself was not immune to his evil machinations.

The Pentateuch is a guide for all people, who seek to know and love the Lord. Later, after the flood, the Lord chose Abraham, as a conduit from which God's holiness could flow. Abraham originally was from Ur, a Mesopotamian city, situated on the banks of the river Euphrates. He then moved on to Canaan, living a nomadic existence, but believing that this was the land that God had promised him and his descendants.

After a sojourn in Egypt of 450 years, where Abraham's descendants multiplied and became a nation, God raised up Moses with his brother Aaron to lead the Hebrews out of Egypt. This journey out of Egypt was named the Exodus, which means 'going out of', which from then on became the key event in the history of the Israelites. From that point on future generations have commemorated this event by the first festival known as the Passover.

Ethical Laws

After travelling for three months in the desert, the Israelites camped before Mount Sinai. It was here that God made a covenant expressing His desire to make them His chosen people. Their part of the covenant was to keep his laws which were summed up in the Ten Commandments. In a ceremony, they confirmed their will to obey all God's rules, which contained His requirements for all humankind – honour and obedience to Him and respect and care for each other.

Ritual Laws

Together with the ethical laws, God set out the patterns of worship, based on animal sacrifice. This first act of worship was enacted by Abel, and then continued throughout all future generations of men of God, until the destruction of the temple.

Although animal sacrifice was also used by the surrounding nations who did not acknowledge the sovereignty of Creator God, this does not in any way reduce the meaning of the bloodshed, which from the beginning was a constant reminder to all people that salvation from sin was only appeased by death.

To the Christians this act of obedience on behalf of the Jews pointed to the coming of the Holy Lamb of God – His Son who came down from heaven to pay the ultimate sacrifice for the sins of the whole world. John testified to this by proclaiming when he spied Jesus coming unto him: *"Behold the Lamb of God, which taketh away the sin of the world"* (John 1:29).

The Lord not only decreed how humans should behave in the tabernacle but set up a hierarchy – the Tribe of Levites, headed by Aaron as the High Priest to guide the Israelites in their communal worship and teach the people.

Christ himself gave us a strong message to observe and continue to live by covenant laws and observe annual celebratory occasions both sacred and festive. These times set apart for the Lord, reinforced the need to 'remember' God's acts of deliverance and continued blessing.

Every year of His life on earth, Jesus observed annual celebrations as part of his worship and teaching about the Father (McNeely, 2014). Some have given the total number as seventeen.

The church, over the centuries, has continued to recognise the Ten Commandments, reciting them in their services. They have also continued to celebrate Christian periods of remembrance and rejoicing – Christmas, Easter, Pentecost, to name a few.

For a Christian, a phrase representing covenant laws, together with other statements of faith is 'The Creed' or in Latin, *Credo*. It became a statement of shared Christian beliefs. The earliest creed in Christianity was 'Jesus is Lord' (Wikipedia – Creed 2021).

This book has described God's holiness and splendour, also instructing people how to respond to it. To the Jews before Christ, He provided civil, ethical, and sacramental instructions. To the Christians, the Pentateuch gives symbolic depth of realities fulfilled and additional impactions for how Christian should live and worship in the light of the new covenant.

As an appropriate conclusion, I quote verses from the hymn of this name: 'Worship the Lord in the beauty of holiness' written by John Samuel Bewley Monsell who was an Anglican priest and poet.

> Worship the Lord in the beauty of holiness,
> Bow down before Him, His glory proclaim;
> Gold of obedience and incense of lowliness
> Kneel and adore Him; the Lord is His name.

> Fear not to enter His courts in the slenderness,
> of the poor wealth thou wouldst reckon as thine.
> Truth in its beauty and love in its tenderness,
> these are the offerings to lay on His shrine.

> Worship the Lord in the beauty of holiness,
> Bow down before Him, His glory proclaim;
> Gold of obedience and incense of lowliness
> Kneel and adore Him: the Lord is His name.

REFERENCES

Ancient Egypt Online (2010). *Song of the Harper* (D. Mackenzie, Trans.). https://ancientegyptonline.co.uk/

Ancient Egyptian Texts. (2020). The songs of Isis and Nephthys (R O Faulkner, Trans.). http://attalus.org/egypt/isis_nephthys.html

Apostolic Constitutions: Book II. New Advent LLC (2021). https://www.newadvent.org/fathers/07152.htm (Original work published 1886)

Appleton, G (1987). *Understanding the Psalms.* Continuum International Publis.

AZ Quotes. (2022). Martin Luther quotes. https://www.azquotes.com/author/9142-Martin_Luther

Berman, J A (2006). God's alliance with man. https://azure.org.il/include/print.php?id=131

Bower, C. M (1966). *Boethius' the principles of music: An introduction, translation, and commentary.* George Peabody College for Teachers.

Britannica, Editors of Encyclopedia (2019). Noahide Laws. https://www.britannica.com/topic/Noahide-Laws

Church of England in Australia. (1985). *An Australian prayer book.* Anglican Information Office.

Clemens, T F (2010). *The writings of Clement of Alexandria* (W Wilson, Trans.). Kessinger Publishing. (Original work published AD 325)

Collins English Dictionary. (2021). *Definition of omniscient.* https://www.collinsdictionary.com/dictionary/english/omniscient

Compelling Truth. (2021). *What does it mean that God is Jehovah-Rapha?* https://www.compellingtruth.org/Jehovah-Rapha.html

Copernicus, N (1999). *De Revolutionibus Orbium Coelestium* (E. Rosen, Trans.). Octavo. (Original work published 1543)

Cunningham, P J (1992). *Exploring scripture: How the Bible came to be.* Paulist Press.

Cyber Hymnal. (2021, Sept 19). *Robert Lowry*. http://www.hymntime.com/tch/bio/l/o/w/r/lowry_r.htm

Davis, C W & Menuhin, Y, (2000). *The music of man: Exploring the miracle of music and its influence throughout the ages*. Methuen.

DeHaan, M R (1955). *The tabernacle: The house of blood*. Zondervan.

Discipleship Ministries. (2013 June 25). *History of hymns: Immortal, invisible, God only wise*. https://www.umcdiscipleship.org/resources/history-of-hymns-immortal-invisible-god-only-wise (Original work published 1867)

Dowley, T (2011). *Christian music: A global history*. Lion Hudson.

Drane, J W (Ed.). (1998). Genesis. In *The new lion encyclopedia of the Bible*. Lion Publishing.

Dunstan, A (1973). *These are the hymns: With some examples of orders for special services*. SPCK Publishing.

Edersheim, A (1994). *The temple: Its ministry and services*. Hendrickson Publishers. (Original work published 1874)

Eerdmans. (1986). Phylactery. In *International standard bible encyclopedia* (p. 864).

Feder, Y (2014). *The significance of Hittite treaties for Biblical studies and Orthodox Judaism*. The Torah.com. https://www.thetorah.com/article/significance-of-hittite-treaties-for-torah-judaism

Finocchiaro, M A (Ed.) (1989). *The Galileo affair: A documentary history*. University of California Press. (Original work published 1615-1633)

Frey, M (2011). *The sabbath in the pentateuch: An exegetical and theological study*. Andrews University Seminary Studies.

Galileo Galilei (2017). In E. N. Zalta (Ed.). *Stanford Encyclopedia of Philosophy*. Department Stanford University Stanford.

Geneva Bible: The Bible of the protestant reformation. (2007). Hendrickson Publishers. (Original work published 1560)

Glaser, M. & Glaser, Z (1987). *The fall feasts of Israel*. Moody Press.

Glaspey, T (2015). *75 Masterpiece: Every christian should know: The fascinating stories behind great works of art, literature, music and film*. Baker Books.

Glynn, P (1996). *Psalms: Songs for the way home.* Marist Fathers Books.
Godwin, M (1990). *Angels: An endangered species.* Simon & Schuster.
Graham, B (1995). *Angels: God's secret agents.* Thomas Nelson.
Griffith, JW (2017). *The three levels of music: The artist's role as a conduit.*
Harwood, R (1984). *All the world's a stage.* Secker & Warburg.
Heber, R (1972). Holy, holy, holy! Lord God Almighty. In *Worshipbook* (#421). Westminster Press. (Original work published 1826)
Hope Publishing Company. (2022). *The Lord made man: The scriptures tell.* https://www.hopepublishing.com/dudley-smith-timothy
Houghton, E (1982). *Christian hymn-writers.* Evangelical Press of Wales.
Hudson, M (2018). *...and forgive them their debts: Lending, foreclosure, and redemption from bronze age finance to the jubilee year.* Islet-Verlag Dresden.
InterVarsity Press (1998). The tabernacle. In *Dictionary of biblical imagery.* (p. 837).
Jerusalem Talmud (1987). Rosh Hashanah 4:9. In M Glaser, & Z Glaser, *The fall feasts of Israel.* Moody Press.
Jewish Virtual Library (1998-2021). *Tractate hagiga: Synopsis of subjects.* https://www.jewishvirtuallibrary.org/synopsis-of-subjects-for-tractate-hagiga
Josephus, F (1987). *The works of Josephus* (W Whiston, Trans.). Hendrickson Publishers. (Original work published 37-38)
Karolyi, O (1981). *Introducing music.* Penguin Books.
Katz, A (2008). *An anatomy of deception.* Burning Bush Publications.
Katz, A (2009). *Apostolic foundations.* Burning Bush Publications.
Kavanaugh, P (1996). *Spiritual lives of the great composers.* Zondervan Publishing House.
Kent, (2022). *The silver scrolls.* Eternity Media Productions.
Kepler, J (1618–21). Epitome Astronomiae Copernicanae (*Epitome of Copernican astronomy*) (C G Wallis, Trans.). Annapolis.
Kilmer, A (2001). *Mesopotamia.* Grove Music Online. https://www.oxfordmusiconline.com/grovemusic

Kirby, P (2022). *Theophilus of Antioch*. Early Christian Writings. http://www.earlychristianwritings.com/text/theophilus-book2.html

Knights, J (1997). *Daniel and...: How to survive in a pagan culture*. John Knights.

LaGard Smith, F (1984). Moses Emerges as Leader. In *The daily bible* (p. 97). Harvest House Publishers.

Lightner, R P (1998). *Angels, Satan, and demons: Invisible beings that inhabit the spiritual world*. Word Publishing.

Lockyer, H. (1995). *All the angels in the bible*. Hendrickson Publishing.

Lockyer, H. Jr (2004). *All the music of the bible*. Hendrickson Publishing.

MacArthur, J. (2005). *The MacArthur Bible commentary*. Thomas Nelson.

Marshall Cavendish. (1983). *The great composers and their music: Handel's messiah (highlights)* Vol. 2, part 23. Marshall Cavendish.

Maxwell, W. D. (1945). *An outline of christian worship: Its development and forms*. Oxford University Press.

McAdoo, H. R. (1991). *Anglican heritage: Theology and spirituality*. Canterbury Press.

McAleer, S. (2020). *Plato's republic: An introduction*. Open Book Publishers.

Menuhin, Y. & Davis, C. W. (1979). *The music of man*. Methuen.

Menuhin, Y. (1977). *The book of music*. New Burlington Books.

Metzger, B. M. (Ed.). (1965). *The Apocrypha of the Old Testament*. Oxford University Press.

Millard, A. (1985). *Treasures from bible times*. Lion Publishing.

Millard, A. (2009). Creation stories. In D. Alexander & P. Alexander (Eds.), *The lion handbook to the bible* (4th ed., pp. 117-118). Lion Publishing.

Milton, J. (1974). Paradise lost. In J. Canning (Ed.), *100 great books: Masterpieces of all time*. (pp. 128-132). Souvenir Press.

Mission Venture Ministries. (13 January 2014). *Jehovah Rapha: The Lord who heals: Exodus 15:26* https://missionventureministries.wordpress.com

My Jewish Learning. (2022). *What is the Talmud?* https://www.myjewishlearning.com/article

Oxford University Press. (1991). Trivium. In *The Oxford Dictionary of English Etymology* (p. 944).

Parris, D P (2006). *Reading the bible with giants: How 2000 years of biblical interpretation can shed new light on old texts.* Paternoster

Pentecost, J D (1997). *Your adversary the devil.* Kregel Publications.

Peterson, J B (2019). *12 rules for life: An antidote to chaos.* Penguin Books.

Pfeiffer, C F (1960). *An outline of Old Testament history.* Moody Press.

Planetary Sciences, (2019). *Black holes.* https://planetary-science.org/astrophysics/black-holes/

Poole, M (1962). *Commentary on the holy Bible, volume 1: Genesis-Job.* Banner of Truth.

Previn, A (Ed.) (1983). *Andre Previn's guide to the orchestra.* Macmillan Publishers.

Reader's Digest Association (1994). Moses. In *Reader Digest Who's who in the bible?* (p. 306)

Reader's Digest Association (1994). Moses. In *Reader Digest Who's who in the bible?* (p. 310)

Richman, C. (1997). *A house of prayer for all nations: The holy temple of Jerusalem.* The Temple Institute & Carta.

Rico, G (2005). Boethius. In S Clark, & E. E. Leach (Eds.), *Citation and authority in medieval and renaissance musical culture.* Boydell Press.

Roberts, J. (1839). *Caniadau y Cyssegr,* The National Library of Wales. https://archives.library.wales/index.php/caniadau-y-cyssegr-2

Rowley, H H (1967). *Worship in ancient Israel: Its forms and meaning.* S.P.C.K.

Russell, D S (1976). *Between the testaments.* SCM Press.

Samuel, D (2009). The music of the spheres. https://www.sensorystudies.org/picture-gallery/spheres_image/

Sapolsky, R M (2004). *Why zebras don't get ulcers.* Henry Holt and Co.

Shakespeare, W (2012). Hamlet. In C. Belsey *Shakespeare in theory and practice.* Cambridge University Press. (Original work published 1595)

Shakespeare, W (2014). Romeo and Juliet. In C. Belsey *Romeo and Juliet language and writing.* Bloomsbury Publishing. (Original work published 1595)

Shaver, D A (Ed.) (2015). *The book of Enoch: The collector's edition* (R. H. Charles, Trans.). CreateSpace Independent Publishing Platform. (Original work published 1917)

Siegel, E (2019, May 29). *This is how, 100 years ago, a solar eclipse proved Einstein right and Newton wrong.* https://www.forbes.com/sites/startswithabang/2019/05/29/this-is-how-100-years-ago-a-solar-eclipse-proved-einstein-right-and-newton-wrong/

Smith, W C (2012). Immortal, invisible, God only wise. In *Indelible grace hymn book*. http://hymnbook.igracemusic.com/hymns/immortal-invisible-god-only-wise (Original work published 1867)

Snow, C P (1967). *Variety of men.* Macmillan.

Sproul, R C (2011). *Unseen realities: Heaven, hell, angels, and demons.* Christian Focus Publications.

Stainer, J.(2018). *The music of the bible.* Novello and Company.

Temple, A (1954). *Hymns we love: Stories of the hundred most popular hymns.* Lutterworth Press.

The Latin Vulgate Bible (St. Jerome, E S Hieronymus, Trans.). (2012). https://vulgate.org/ot/job_38.htm (Original work published 382 AD)

The scripture of the dead sea sect (T. H. Gaster, Trans.) (1956). Secker & Warburg. (Original work published 170 BC/68 AD)

Thomas Nelson (1995). Star. In *Nelson's new illustrated bible dictionary* (2nd ed., p. 1201).

University of Cambridge, (2022). *Professor Andrew Fabian; Professor at Institute of Astronomy, University of Cambridge.* https://www.csap.cam.ac.uk/network/andrew-fabian/

Venerable St Joseph the hymnographer. (2022). Russian orthodox cathedral of St John the Baptist. https://stjohndc.org/en/orthodoxy-foundation/saints/venerable-st-joseph-hymnographer

Viney, L. (2018, August 17). Good vibrations: The role of music in Einstein's thinking. https://www.abc.net.au/classic/features/good-vibrations-the-role-of-music-in-einsteins-thinking/10127100

Warner Wallace, J (2018, August 17). Is the astronomy in the book of Job scientifically consistent? *Cold-case christianity.* https://coldcasechristianity.com/writings/is-the-astronomy-in-the-book-of-job-scientifically-consisten

Wilmington, D(1985). *Wilmington's guide to the Bible.* Tyndale House Publishers.

Wilson, C & Wilson, B (1999). *The stones still shout: Sensational highlights of the bible and archaeology.* Pacific Christian Ministries.

Wilson-Dickson, A (2003). *The story of christian music: From Gregorian chant to black gospel: An authoritative illustrated guide to all the major traditions of music for worship.* Lion Publication.

Zeitler, W(2022). *Allthescales.org.* https://allthescales.org/

Introduction to the Author

Lois Sonsie-Beel

M.A. T.Mus.A Singing, A.Mus.A. Piano Teaching. Dip. Theology.

Lois Sonsie-Beel has spent her life bringing music to many who may not otherwise have had the opportunity to achieve these skills. During her musical training, she took time to complete a Diploma of Theology and spent a few years working with underprivileged young people, as a Mission Sister, at the Melbourne City Mission. Lois, together with other musicians, flew out to rural areas of Queensland, conducting workshops for church organists and choristers in the finer art of Worship Music. Lois has had an eclectic musical career which included working in universities, schools, churches, and theatre. She also ran a theatre company, with an orchestra, to inspire young people to extend their musical ability.

www.ingramcontent.com/pod-product-compliance
Lightning Source LLC
Chambersburg PA
CBHW031232290426
44109CB00012B/255